SATYAJIT RAY

OUR FILMS
THEIR FILMS

Orient Longman

RAY: OUR FILMS THEIR FILMS

ORIENT LONGMAN PRIVATE LIMITED

Registered Office
3-6-752 Himayatnagar, Hyderabad 500 029 (A.P.), INDIA
e-mail: cogeneral@orientlongman.com

Other Offices
Bangalore, Bhopal, Bhubaneshwar, Chennai, Ernakulam, Guwahati,
Hyderabad, Jaipur, Kolkata, Lucknow, Mumbai, New Delhi, Patna

First Published 1976
Third edition 1993
Reprinted 1998, 2001, 2003, 2005, 2006, 2007

ISBN 13: 978 81 250 1565 9
ISBN 10: 81 250 1565 5

Printed in India at
Sai Printopack Pvt Ltd
New Delhi

Published by
Orient Longman Private Limited
1/24 Asaf Ali Road
New Delhi 110 002
e-mail: delgeneral@orientlongman.com

Contents 🖋

Acknowledgements ✍

I wish to thank Mr R. N. Das who first suggested that I put together in a book my talks and articles on the cinema. This was in 1971, when Mr Das was the manager of Orient Longman, Calcutta.

I am grateful to the publishers for bearing with me through the long period of gestation. The blame for the delay rests squarely on my shoulders. I had been careless in preserving my own published writings, most of which lay scattered in the pages of film journals, film club bulletins, daily newspapers and various other periodicals.

Thanks are due to the late Nemai Ghosh (of *Chhinnamul* fame) and Shri Sunit Sen Gupta for their invaluable help in retrieving some of the more elusive pieces.

Finally, a special word of thanks to Shri Nirmalya Acharya for helping the book along at every stage, from its inception to its emergence as a finished entity.

S.R.

The author and the publishers wish to acknowledge the following newspapers and periodicals in which the articles and lectures, excepting the 'Introduction', first appeared:

The Statesman, Indian Film Culture, Sight and Sound, International Film Annual, New York Times, Seminar, Montage, Star and Style, Amrita Bazar Patrika, Filmfare, Sequence, Calcutta Film Society Bulletin, Show, Kino, Now, Hindusthan Standard, and *Span.*

Introduction ✍

A film maker rarely writes about films. He is either too busy making one, or too unhappy not to be able to make one, or too exhausted from the last one he made. Cocteau could write a film maker's diary because he was a sort of superior dabbler who never knew the sustained pressures of professional film making. Eisenstein used words as copiously as he used celluloid; but then he was a teacher and a theoretician as much as a film maker. Others have written about their films at the end of their careers. But by and large film makers have desisted from adding footnotes to their own work.

This reticence has encouraged the growth of a mystique which has helped the film maker to sustain his ego while concealing his vulnerability. His ego is an indispensable part of his equipment. With vast amounts of money at his disposal and a whole army of talents at his beck and call, he must work with a far greater sense of power than any other artist in any other field. The very word 'Action' with which he gets a scene going has the authentic ring of an army command. Indeed, he knows well that as long as the film is in the making, he is the one who is expected to dominate.

But once the making is over, the sense of power evaporates and helplessness creeps in. He realises that he is not only answerable to critics, which all artists are, but to the

man who provided the wherewithal, and to the faceless
millions who form the public pulse which must now beat
with his film for the film itself not to fall by the wayside
and die. No wonder the film maker is reduced to a state
of mute resignation. All he can do is wait for the next
film to restore his ego by handing him back his mantle of
authority.

It is only in recent years that film makers have begun to
show signs of being articulate. Not in writing, though, and
not on their own. Indefatigable critics armed with tape
recorders have coaxed them out of their retreats, cajoled
them into speech and faithfully recorded and transcribed
every word. For obvious reasons, only directors with marked
individualities and large followings have been chosen for
this purpose. If this has not led to a full-scale revelation
of the mysteries of creation, it has at least given some
interesting glimpses of their working methods, and by so
doing led to a partial demystification of the film making
process.

A sort of reverse phenomenon has also taken place in
recent times. Quite a number of film critics have given up
writing and switched over to film making. In France in the
late fifties a whole group of young critics from *Cahiers du
Cinéma* left their desks and started a now-celebrated film
movement. Similar things have also happened in Britain
and elsewhere. It is interesting to observe that once the
transition was made few went back to writing again.

If I had my choice, most of the pieces in this book
would not have been written at all. They are the outcomes
of promises for articles and talks given at unguarded
moments to various magazines and organisations. This is
not to say that I regret having written them. In the unique
circumstances in which films are made in Bengal, some
accounts of my experiences and working methods may have

some value, at least for those in our country who would tread the same path but are not aware of the pitfalls.

Some of the problems a film maker faces are of a general nature, where one man's solutions would do for all. More often than not, a film brings with it its own unique set of stumbling blocks. Some may be disposed of easily, others may call for effort. Yet others may prove wholly intractable. These usually end up by clinging tenaciously to the film as blemishes which the director fervently hopes will not be noticed.

A lesson I have learnt and have been at pains not to conceal is that film making is by far the most physically demanding of all activities that are dignified by the epithet 'creative'. The whole process takes place in three broad stages: writing, filming and editing. All three are creative; but while in the first and the third one uses mainly one's head, the second calls for the use of all one's faculties—cerebral, physical and emotional—going full steam at all times. Any film maker who while at work bears any resemblance to the popular conception of the artist as a withdrawn individual in rapt communion with his Muse is obviously shirking and has no business to be within miles of a movie camera.

And yet to one who survives the initial shock of unrelenting pressure, film making offers rewards as nothing else does. I hope I have been able to convey in my writings some of the unique excitement I get out of my work.

The second part of the book is mainly concerned with foreign films. I have been making films for twenty-two years. Before that, for about the same length of time, I had looked at other people's films, mostly from other countries, mainly American. In my childhood, visits to the cinema

were big, if infrequent, occasions filled with the delights
of the latest Chaplin or Keaton or Harold Lloyd. This was
followed, in the early years of sound, by a Laurel-and-
Hardy phase, a Tarzan phase and a swashbuckling adventure phase. When I was fifteen or so, I earned the right to
choose my own diet. This led to a great opening up of the
vista. Westerns, gangster films, horror films, musicals,
comedies, dramas and all those other species which Hollywood served up with such expertise, came tumbling my
way to be lapped up with ever-increasing appetite. I noted
each title in a little pocket diary, adding brief critical
comments, and my own star rating.

The addiction persisted through college, with one important change of attitude: the stars gave way to directors as
my focus of interest. I had earlier learned to recognise the
hallmarks of the major Hollywood studios. I could make
out an MGM film from a Paramount one, or a Warner's
production from a 20th Century Fox one, by the distinctive
quality of finish which each major studio took special care
to put on its products. It was described by the word 'mounting', and it was fun to try and make out what this mounting
consisted of. This now gave way to a study of the hallmarks of directors. In what way was Ford different from
Wyler, or Wyler from Capra, or Capra from Stevens?
This was precisely the point where my interest took a serious turn. It had suddenly dawned on me that more than
the studio, more than the stars, more than the story, it was
the director who gave a distinguished film its mark of distinction.

After college and graduation, I went to Santiniketan for
a course in Fine Arts. I had vague plans for a career in graphic arts. I had a flair for drawing but needed a foundation
of discipline to be able to make any use of it. With me
went my small but precious collection of gramophone re-

cords of classical western music. I needed my second love
because, in leaving the city, I was leaving my first love behind. As it turned out, the only cinema in the vicinity of the
campus was two miles away, had wooden benches for seats,
and showed mythological films. This put me in the dol-
drums until I discovered in the shelves of the arts department library three books on the cinema. They were Rotha's
Film Till Now, and the two books of theory by Arnheim
and Spottiswoode.

I left Santiniketan in the middle of the first spate of
Japanese air raids over Calcutta in the winter of 1942. Six
months after my return home I got a job as a visualiser in
a British-owned advertising agency. Calcutta now being a
base of operations in the war, Chowringhee was chock-a-
block with GIs. The pavement book stalls displayed wafer-
thin editions of *Life* and *Time*, and the jam-packed cinemas showed the very latest films from Hollywood. While I
sat at my office desk sketching out campaigns for tea and
biscuits, my mind buzzed with the thoughts of the films I
had been seeing. I never ceased to regret that while I had
stood in the scorching summer sun in the wilds of Santiniketan sketching *simul* and *palash* in full bloom, *Citizen
Kane* had come and gone, playing for just three days in the
newest and biggest cinema in Calcutta.

Although Hollywood struck an extraordinarily rich vein
at this time, and my film going had never been more frequent nor more richly rewarding, I felt only partially educated. All those great names in French and German and
Soviet cinema stared at me from the pages of *Sight and
Sound*, but there was no way I could get to see them.
Luckily some of the great film makers of Europe had in the
meantime migrated to Hollywood, and I was soon thrilled
to encounter my first Hollywood-Renoir and my first Holly-
wood-Clair. This was followed by a sudden influx of Soviet

films. I shall never forget the day I saw the first part of *Ivan the Terrible*, on a Sunday morning in a North Calcutta cinema. The Gothic gloom of the film, Cherkasov's grand gestures, and the music of Prokofiev stayed with me all through the day and well into the night, until I fell asleep and found them back in a grotesque dream, in the middle of which I woke up gasping for breath. It turned out that a *paan* I had bought from a shop next to the cinema had given me quinsy, swelling the inside of my throat to the point where I could barely breathe.

By the time the war ended, I had taken out subscriptions to most of the film magazines in the English language and snapped up every film book I could lay my hands on. One of my most valued acquisitions was a second-hand copy of the screenplay of René Clair's British film, *The Ghost Goes West*. This was my first encounter with a film script, and it gave me the idea to start writing screenplays as a pastime.

In the year of India's independence we formed the first film club in Calcutta, thereby shackling ourselves willingly to the task of disseminating film culture amongst the intelligentsia. In my job I was now firmly established not only as a visualiser, but also as an illustrator and a designer of book jackets. In all this time the thought had not once occurred to me of changing my profession. Graphics were my bread and butter, while films were food for the mind, as music was too. My three years in Santiniketan had opened my eyes and ears to our artistic and musical heritage, so that in addition to buying records of symphonies and concertos, I was now regularly going to concerts of Indian classical music.

For the first two years of its existence, the membership

of our club refused to go above twenty-five. Our enthusiasm was beginning to acquire a tinge of cynicism. We could see we did not have much of a field to disseminate over. We were also being subjected to a two-pronged attack. One came from the film trade, which spread the word that a group of subversive youngsters was running down Bengali films at meetings and seminars. The other came from a household which included one of our club members. It was an isolated case, but may well have been a typical one. This member had offered us the use of his drawing room for one of our meetings. Since we did not have a regular club room, members took turns to provide facilities in their own houses. On this occasion, in the middle of our discussion, our friend was summoned by the owner of the house and summarily told that he would not put up with film people spoiling the sanctity of his house. We were thrown out of the place.

I now decided to spread our gospel over a wider field. I wrote an article on Bengali films which came out in one of the leading English dailies of Calcutta. I had thought my explosive piece would shake the Bengali cinema to its foundations and lead to a massive heart-searching among our film makers. Nothing of the sort happened. The piece was simply shrugged off by the people of the trade as yet another piece of tomfoolery by some arrogant upstart who saw only foreign films and knew nothing of local needs and local conditions.

But if the trade itself ignored my article, there were others on the fringe of it who did not. A few days after it came out, I got a phone call from a well-known screen writer who was about to start an ambitious new film which he would direct himself. He said he wished to see me about his film, adding that he had admired my article almost as much as he admired my book jackets. We made an appoint-

ment, and I turned up in his office the next day. With irre-
proachable logic, he offered me the job of art director on
his new film. Even if I felt a little deflated, I did not have
the heart to pass up an opportunity to find out what 'local
conditions' were really like. And I felt this was something
I could handle in my spare time without having to give up
my regular job. I accepted his offer, attended the first story
conference, came back home and started making sketches
of the sets. A week later, word came that the job had been
given to a well-known painter with a flair for interior de-
coration.

The second offer pleased me more. One of the screenplays I had turned out in my spare time was based on a
short story by a well-known Bengali writer. It concerned an
overbearing English manager of a zemindari estate whose
dark doings are brought to an end by a plucky Bengali
youth with radical leanings. The treatment was read by a
friend of mine who recommended it to a businessman-
acquaintance who was thinking of producing a film. Soon I
was summoned in the businessman's presence and asked to
read out the treatment. I sat down on one side of the longest conference table I had ever seen, and had to turn my
chair at an angle to face the businessman who occupied the
head. Across the table, facing me directly, sat a professional
cameraman who had been trained at UFA in the days of
Pabst and Murnau. Behind me, peering over my shoulder,
sat a well-known director with many hits to his credit. I
opened my script and started my recital. I had scarcely
finished the first scene when I felt a tap on my shoulder. 'How
many climaxes do you have in your story?' asked the maker
of hits. I could see that he had designs to nip me in the
bud if I named a lower figure than the one he presumably
prescribed as the obligatory minimum for a potential hit.
I said I had not counted, but he was free to work it out as

the story unfolded. Fortunately no further taps intruded
the reading of my screenplay. When I finished the producer
said he liked the story very much, and had only one small
suggestion to make: in the final scene of confrontation,
where the hero gives the now cringing English manager
a piece of his mind, his words should end with the per-
emptory exhortation: 'Quit India.' The film was never
made.

In 1949, Jean Renoir came to Calcutta to scout locations
for *The River*. Based on the talks I had with him, I wrote
an article. When the English magazine *Sequence* published
it, the thought occurred to me to take up film journalism
as a sideline. I had two more subjects in mind: one on the
nature and function of background music, the other on an
Orson Welles film I had seen recently. I hoped to make a
major contribution to film criticism by demonstrating that
in *The Lady From Shanghai*, Welles had made the first
'atonal' film in the history of the cinema. Neither one ever
got written. In April of the following year, my wife and I
left India on a P & O liner bound for England. I was to
work for six months in London in my agency's head office.
Doubtless the management hoped that I would come back
a full-fledged advertising man wholly dedicated to the pursuit of selling tea and biscuits.

What the trip did in fact was to set the seal of doom
on my advertising career. Within three days of arriving
in London I saw *Bicycle Thieves*. I knew immediately that
if I ever made *Pather Panchali*—and the idea had been
at the back of my mind for some time—I would make it
in the same way, using natural locations and unknown
actors.

All through my stay in London, the lessons of *Bicycle*

Thieves and neo-realist cinema stayed with me. On the way
back I drafted out my first treatment of *Pather Panchali*.
That it did not get going until two years later, and did not
get finished until two more, was not for any lack of enthusiasm on my part.

For the next twenty years, whatever I wrote on the
cinema—and I wrote both in Bengali and English—concerned either my own films or films of other countries. In
writing about my own work, I have realised why film
makers have written so little about film making. So complex is the process, so intricate and elusive the triangular
relationship between the maker, the machines and the
human material that is deployed, that to describe even a
single day's work in all its details of conception, collaboration and execution would call for abilities beyond most film
makers. Even with such gifts, a lot of what goes on in the
dark recesses of the film maker's mind would go unsaid,
for the simple reason that it cannot be put into words. In
reading afresh my account of the first day's shooting of
Pather Panchali, I realise I had barely touched on the problems I faced or the lessons I learnt. Some of these lessons
came in strange, oblique ways. Let me give an instance.
One of the shots I had to take on the first day was of the
girl Durga observing her brother Apu—who is unaware
of her presence—from behind a cluster of tall, swaying
reeds. I had planned on a medium close-up with a normal
lens, showing her from waist upwards. We had with us on
that day a friend who was a professional cameraman.
While I stood behind the reeds explaining to Durga what
she had to do in the shot, I had a fleeting glimpse of our
friend fiddling with lenses. What he had done was take
out the normal lens from the camera and substitute one
with a long focal length. 'Just take a look at her with this
one,' he told me, as I came to have a look through the

viewfinder. I had done a lot of still photography before, but in my unswerving allegiance to Cartier-Bresson, I had never worked with a long lens. What the finder now revealed was an enormous close-up of Durga's face, backlit by the sun and framed by the swaying, shimmering reeds she had parted with her hands. It was irresistible. I thanked my friend for his timely advice and took the shot. A few days later, in the cutting room, I was horrified to discover that the scene simply did not call for such an emphatic close-up. For all its beauty, or perhaps because of it, the shot stood out in blatant isolation from its companions, and thereby spoilt the scene. This taught me, at one stroke, two fundamental lessons of film making: (*a*) a shot is beautiful only if it is right in its context, and this rightness has little to do with what appears beautiful to the eye; and (*b*) never listen to advice on details from someone who does not have the whole film in his head as clearly as you do.

And these are not the only lessons I learnt on that fateful first day. In fact, on every full day that I have worked on a film in the twenty years since I left my advertising job, some glimmer of light has revealed some small hidden mystery of the infinitely complex process that is film making.

One of the things I have aimed at constantly in all these years is economy of expression. In Santiniketan, as a student of painting, I had been drawn towards far-eastern calligraphy, which goes to the heart of perceived reality and expresses it by means of minimal brush strokes applied with maximum discipline. In films, the maker is concerned both with what one sees and what one hears. In human terms, this is reduced to action and speech. These are bound up with a character's social identity as well as his individual identity at a given point in a given story. The convincing portrayal of character through speech and action is the combined task of writer, actor and director. It is because the director has the last word on what should appear on the screen that his responsibility exceeds that of the other participants. He is the one who finally decides what looks right and sounds right, and the measure of truth he achieves is in direct ratio to his depth of observation. Looking at *Pather Panchali* today, I am upset by errors of detail which keep blurring the social identity of some of its characters. I know this was caused by my lack of familiarity with the rural scene. And yet it is possible for a film to work, as *Pather Panchali* does, whenever it leaves its regional moorings and rises to a plane of universal gestures and universal emotions. Of course, it is possible to do away wholly with this bothersome aspect of social identification. In fact, this is exactly what the vast majority of Hindi films do, and which accounts for their country-wide acceptance. They present a synthetic, non-existent society, and one can speak of credibility only within the norms of this make-believe world.

The reason why I keep writing about films from time to time is that perhaps at the back of my mind there are still remnants of the zeal to spread film culture that brought our film club into being. And there are provocations too. While it is true that inadequate technical resources, erratic financing, slackness in writing and direction and acting, have all contributed to the generally poor quality of films that surround us, I have no doubt that equal harm has been done by critics—which, in films, mean anybody with access to print—who keep peddling muddled notions about the art form. On two occasions I have been provoked to write in self-defence against attacks for deviating from literary originals. Obviously, what these critics expected were literal translations—impossible where a change of medium is involved—rather than interpretations. One of the two attacks, published in a Bengali monthly, was aimed at *Charulata*. I hastened to write back at great length justifying in cinematic terms every liberty I had taken. Doubtless the seed fell on barren ground. Because even to this day, a film maker who takes up a classic, sticks to the letter, but wholly misses the spirit, arouses little indignation. This is surely the result of lop-sided film education, of lack of connoisseurship, and applies only to a country which took one of the greatest inventions of the West with the most far-reaching artistic potential, and promptly cut it down to size.

In the West, the cinema has seen some clearly marked periods of revolution, in the course of which certain norms developed and conventions solidified. Occasionally, the discovery of a major new trend—such as neo-realism in the forties—or a new school of film making—such as the Japanese in the fifties—has led to some critical rethinking, but on the whole the larger truths have survived. Even New Wave did not wholly change the face of the cinema. It only enlarged its vocabulary and dislodged some hallowed bricks from the edifice of film grammar. To most films now made in Europe and elsewhere, the norms still apply. It is only in the case of an occasional highly personal work that the critic has to take refuge in total subjectivity.

What I consider a far greater revolution has taken place on the level of content. This is a phenomenon of the sixties, and is described by the term permissiveness. In the beginning, it was marked by a freedom in the treatment of eroticism. Latterly, this freedom has grown to embrace just about every bodily activity the camera is capable of recording. A great deal has been written to condone permissive-

ness as marking the end of the prudery that has, according
to its proponents, besmirched and falsified mores from
their inception right up to the time the audience had their
first glimpse of pubic hair in a public cinema. Apart from
its insolent implication that artists like Renoir, Carné, Clair,
Stroheim, Dreyer, De Sica, Pabst, Mizoguchi (make up
your own list of past greats)—all falsified human relationships in their films, the view errs in discounting the
power of suggestion which is inherent in all art and is a pre-
rogative of all artists. There is no doubt that permissiveness
in the cinema is of major sociological significance as a reflection of the changing mores of Western society; but to
justify it as some higher form of artistic truth is as ridicu-
lous as the simulated intercourse indulged in by unclothed
performers in film after film after permissive film. Apparently, such is the dread in which the stigma of prudery is
held in the West today that even the distinction between
gratuitous eroticism, which is plain pornography, and eroticism that is valid in its context, is glossed over by most
critics.

There is yet another phenomenon of major significance
to which I must allude before I close. This has to do with
film books and film magazines. When I first began to take
a serious interest in films, I could have possessed, without
much strain on my purse, all the English books on the art
of the cinema, and shoved them all comfortably on to a
single shelf of my book case. Today, I have a comprehen-
sive catalogue of film books in the English language which
runs to over three hundred pages. Of magazines one has
lost count. In Calcutta, most bookshops in the heart of the
city display film books which are picked up well before they
have gathered dust. The number of film clubs in the city

20

has crossed the dozen mark and keeps increasing. Most clubs come out with their own seasonal bulletins and have their own panels of critics. What used to be esoteric film terms are now part of everyday speech. Ask any man of average education if he knows the meaning of 'freeze', and the chances are he will not only give the right answer but back it up with appropriate examples. Tickets for festivals of foreign films are swooped up in no time regardless of whether the films belong to a pre-permissive or post-permissive era. The greats of the cinema are no longer just names in the pages of *Sight and Sound* and history books. They are now part of the local film scene, setting up periodic ripples, sending the critics to their desks and their dissertations.

Is all this, then, a presage of something bright, something hopeful and positive? Something that will lift the gloom and change the face of our films? I wish I could believe so. But the rude fact is, cinema has never been saved by writers. We may· have more of them now than ever before, but at the same time there are more and stronger shoulders now to shrug them off. No. Words are not enough. Words need the backing of action, or there is no revolution. And the only action that counts is that which a film maker calls into play by snapping out his word of command in his own particular field of battle. If his victory, and of many others like him, restore even a little of the dignity a great art form has lost, only then can we talk of having a revolution.

OUR FILMS

What is Wrong with Indian Films?

One of the most significant phenomena of our time has been the development of the cinema from a-turn-of-the-century mechanical toy into the century's most potent and versatile art form. In its early chameleon-like phase the cinema was used variously as an extension of photography, as a substitute for the theatre and the music hall, and as part of the magician's paraphernalia. By the twenties, the cynics and know-alls had stopped smirking and turned down their noses.

Today, the cinema commands the respect accorded to any other form of creative expression. In the immense complexity of its creative process, it combines in various measures the functions of poetry, music, painting, drama, architecture and a host of other arts, major and minor. It also combines the cold logic of science with the subtlest abstractions of the human imagination. No matter what goes into the making of it, no matter who uses it and how —a producer for financial profits, a political body for propaganda or an *avant-garde* intellectual for the satisfaction of an aesthetic urge—the cinema is basically the expression of a concept or concepts in aesthetic terms; terms which have crystallised through the incredibly short years of its existence.

It was perhaps inevitable that the cinema should have found the greatest impetus in America. A country without any deep-rooted cultural and artistic traditions was perhaps best able to appraise the new medium objectively. Thanks to pioneers like Griffith, and to the vast sensation-mongering public with its constant clamour for something new, the basic style of film making was evolved and the tools for its production perfected much quicker than would be normally possible. The cinema has now attained a stage where it can handle Shakespeare and psychiatry with equal facility. Technically, in the black and white field, the cinema is supremely at ease. Newer developments in colour and three-dimensional photography are imminent, and it is possible that before the decade is out, the aesthetics of film making will have seen far-reaching changes.

Meanwhile, 'studios sprang up,' to quote an American writer in *Screenwriter*, 'even in such unlikely lands as India and China'. One may note in passing that this springing up has been happening in India for nearly forty years. For a country so far removed from the centre of things, India took up film production surprisingly early. The first short was produced in 1907 and the first feature in 1913. By the twenties it had reached the status of big business.

It is easy to tell the world that film production in India is quantitatively second only to Hollywood; for that is a statistical fact. But can the same be said of its quality? Why are our films not shown abroad? Is it solely because India offers a potential market for her own products? Perhaps the symbolism employed is too obscure for foreigners? Or are we just plain ashamed of our films?

To anyone familiar with the relative standards of the best foreign and Indian films, the answers must come easily. Let us face the truth. There has yet been no Indian film which could be acclaimed on all counts. Where other countries have achieved, we have only attempted and that too not always with honesty, so that even our best films have to be accepted with the gently apologetic proviso that it is 'after all an Indian film'.

No doubt this lack of maturity can be attributed to several factors. The producers will tell you about that mysterious entity 'the mass', which 'goes in for this sort of thing', the technicians will blame the tools and the director will have much to say about the wonderful things he had in mind but could not achieve because of 'the conditions'. These protestations are true but not to the extent you are asked to believe. In any case, better things have been achieved under much worse conditions. The internationally acclaimed post-war Italian cinema is a case in point. The reason lies elsewhere. I think it will be found in the fundamentals of film making.

In the primitive state films were much alike, no matter where they were produced. As the pioneers began to sense the uniqueness of the medium, the language of the cinema gradually evolved. And once the all-important function of the cinema—e.g. movement—was grasped, the sophistication of style and content, and refinement of technique were only a matter of time. In India it would seem that the fundamental concept of a coherent dramatic pattern existing in time was generally misunderstood.

Often by a queer process of reasoning, movement was equated with action and action with melodrama. The analogy with music failed in our case because Indian music is largely improvisational.

This elementary confusion, plus the influence of the American cinema are the two main factors responsible for the present state of Indian films. The superficial aspects of the American style, no matter how outlandish the content, were imitated with reverence. Almost every passing phase of the American cinema has had its repercussion on the Indian film. Stories have been written based on Hollywood successes and the clichés preserved with care. Even where the story has been a genuinely Indian one, the background music has revealed an irrepressible penchant for the jazz idiom.

In the adaptations of novels, one of two courses has been followed: either the story has been distorted to conform to the Hollywood formula, or it has been produced with such devout faithfulness to the original that the purpose of a filmic interpretation has been defeated.

It should be realised that the average American film is a bad model, if only because it depicts a way of life so utterly at variance with our own. Moreover, the high technical polish which is the hallmark of the standard Hollywood product, would be impossible to achieve under existing Indian conditions. What the Indian cinema needs today is not more gloss, but more imagination, more integrity, and a more intelligent appreciation of the limitations of the medium.

After all, we do possess the primary tools of film making. The complaint of the technicians notwithstanding, mechanical devices such as the crane shot and the process shot are useful, but by no means indispensable. In fact, what tools we have, have been used on occasion with real intelligence. What our cinema needs above everything else is a style, an idiom, a sort of iconography of cinema, which would be uniquely and recognisably Indian.

There are some obstacles to this, particularly in the representation of the contemporary scene. The influence of Western civilisation has created anomalies which are apparent in almost every aspect of our life. We accept the motor car, the radio, the telephone, streamlined architecture, European costume, as functional elements of our existence. But within the limits of the cinema frame, their incongruity is sometimes exaggerated to the point of burlesque. I recall a scene in a popular Bengali film which shows the heroine weeping to distraction with her arms around a wireless—an object she associates in her mind with her estranged lover who was once a radio singer.

Another example, a typical Hollywood finale, shows the heroine speeding forth in a sleek convertible in order to catch up with her frustrated lover who has left town on foot; as she sights her man, she abandons the car in a sort of symbolic gesture and runs up the rest of the way to meet him.

The majority of our films are replete with such 'visual dissonances'. In *Kalpana*, Uday Shankar used such dissonances in a conscious and consistent manner so that they became part of his cinematic style. But the truly Indian film should steer clear of such inconsistencies and look for its material in the more basic aspects of Indian life, where habit and speech, dress and manners, background and foreground, blend into a harmonious whole.

It is only in a drastic simplification of style and content that hope for the Indian cinema resides. At present, it would appear that nearly all the prevailing practices go against such simplification.

Starting a production without adequate planning, sometimes even without a shooting script; a penchant for convolutions of plot and counter-plot rather than the strong, simple unidirectional narrative; the practice of sandwiching musical numbers in the most unlyrical situations; the habit of shooting indoors in a country which is all landscape, and at a time when all other countries are turning to the documentary for inspiration—all these stand in the way of the evolution of a distinctive style.

There have been rare glimpses of an enlightened approach in a handful of recent films. IPTA's *Dharti ke Lal* is an instance of a strong simple theme put over with style,

honesty and technical competence. Shankar's *Kalpana,* an
inimitable and highly individual experiment, shows a grasp
of filmic movement, and a respect for tradition which lifts
its best moments to the peak of cinematic achievement.
The satisfying photography which marks the UN documentaries of Paul Zils shows what a discerning camera can do
with the Indian landscape.

The raw material of the cinema is life itself. It is incredible that a country which has inspired so much painting
and music and poetry should fail to move the film maker.
He has only to keep his eyes open, and his ears. Let him
do so.

1948

Extracts from a Banaras Diary ✍

March 1, 1956—Set out at 5 a.m. to explore the ghats.
Half an hour to sunrise, yet more light than one would
have thought, and more activity. The earliest bathers come
about 4 a.m., I gather. The pigeons not active yet, but the
wrestlers are. Incomparable 'atmosphere'. One just wants
to go on absorbing it, being chastened and invigorated
by it. The thought of having to work—planning, picking
sites and extras, setting up camera and microphone, staging
action—is worrying. But here, if anywhere, is a truly *inspiring* setting. It is not enough to say that the ghats are
wonderful or exciting or unique. One must get down to
analysing the reasons for their uniqueness, their impact.
The more you probe, the more is revealed, and the more
you know what to include in your frame and what to leave
out.

In the afternoon the same ghats present an utterly different aspect. Clusters of immobile widows make white patches
on the greyish ochre of the broad steps. The bustle of ablu-
tion is absent. And the light is different, importantly so. The
ghats face east. In the morning they get the full frontal
light of the sun, and the feeling of movement is heightened
by the play of cast shadows. By 4 p.m. the sun is behind
the tall buildings whose shadows now reach the opposite
bank. Result: a diffused light until sunset perfectly in tune
with the subdued nature of the activity.

Morning scenes in the ghat must be shot in the morning and afternoon scenes in the afternoon.

March 2—Explored the lanes in the Bengalitola. Those of Ganesh Mohalla are perhaps the most photogenic. What makes them so?—The curves in the lanes, the breaks in the facades of the houses, the pattern created by the doors, windows, railings, verandas, columns . . . here the light is qualitatively unvarying, and one could pass off a morning shot as an afternoon one.

We chat with the people of the neighbourhood and they promise cooperation. Where would we be without it? We are in fact at the mercy of the residents here and must deal with them with the utmost caution. The smallest *faux pas* and the whole arduous enterprise may be wrecked.

March 3—Called on the Mohant Laxminarayan of the Viswanath Temple. The purpose was to persuade him to give us facilities for shooting inside the temple (something which had never been done before). Pandey, our intermediary, had insisted that I shouldn't be reticent but should 'project my personality', which he was sure would clinch the deal. Two things stood in the way: (*a*) my lack of chaste Hindi and the Mohant's lack of any other language, and (*b*) the fact that the chairs we were given to sit upon had been designed for the maximum comfort of bugs.

It seems at least two more visits will be required before the great Mohant condescends to give a nod of that immobile head of his.

Stopped on our way back at the temple. Were told we were in time for the Saptarshi Arati. A spine-tingling experience. Those who miss it miss one of the great audio-visual treats. Pity I can't use it in any except a decorative manner in the present film. . . .

March 4—Visited the Durga Temple. People who come here with the intent of offering a prayer to the deity usually do so with half a mind, the other half being on the monkeys. These animals go about the place as if they owned it. Irresistibly funny, they sometimes go for your bag of peanuts with alarming viciousness. But when they swing from the bell-ropes and perform an impromptu *carillon*, the sight and sound are no longer merely comic.

Rich possibility of a scene here, with Apu.

March 8—Worked on the script. The opening is a problem, always is. Long shots establishing locale are a cliché. But should one entirely dispense with them in a film which opens in Banaras? The urge not to do so is strong.

As in *Pather Panchali*, I find it has helped in not having a tight script. Working in these circumstances one must leave a lot of room for improvisation within the framework of a broad scheme which one must keep in one's head.

March 15—At the ghats at 5 a.m. to shoot the pigeons. Memorable fiasco. The shot was to be of the pigeons taking flight in a body from their perch on the cornices and making enormous circular sweeps in the sky, as is the way with them. We had a fairly potent-looking bomb which we meant to explode to set the pigeons flying. The camera was set up and Subir had set the match to the fuse when, with barely half a minute to go, Nimai started making frantic but indefinable gestures. We could sense something was wrong, and Subir made an eloquently mimed appeal to the bomb to refrain from exploding. The bomb went off, the pigeons performed nobly, but the camera didn't turn. And then we discovered that the motor had not been connected to the battery.

Luckily, after three or four sweeps the pigeons were back on their perch, and with the second bomb (we had four) we had our shot.

Took the 9 o'clock train to Moghulsarai. Ramani Babu (seventy-year-old resident of Banaras we picked up on the ghat) with us to play Uncle Bhabataran; also Karuna and Pinky. Shooting inside a third class compartment. Sarbajaya and Apu leave Banaras with Bhabataran. Train crosses bridge. S and A look out of window. B eats an orange, spits pips out of window. We give the old man an orange but he consumes it before the camera is ready, so we give him another. Shot is O.K. subject to the Tri-X performing as expected.

March 20—Shot scene of Harihar's collapse on the steps of Chowshati Ghat. Very satisfactory work. A strong wind ruffled the surface of the river and lent movement to the shots. Kanu Babu fell most realistically, got a nasty cut in the knee.

Bloated dead body in the river close to bank and camera. Bathers unperturbed. Probably a common sight.

March 22—5.30 a.m. Started with shot of Apu fetching water from the river. The idea was to have a long shot with Apu in the foreground and a solitary wrestler in the far background, and no other figures. But bathers had already arrived and we had a tough time persuading them to stay out of water, and out of camera-field, until end of shot.

From the ghats to the lanes. Concluding shots of scene of Apu playing hide-and-seek with friends. Clearing the lanes of unwanted elements (animate and inanimate) for long shots a Herculean task. Pack up at 4 p.m. and proceed directly to the Viswanath Temple for shots and recording of *Arati*.

Durga sets up tape recorder in a house across the lane opposite the temple. Mrinal worms his way through milling crowd of devotees with mike and 90 ft. cable which just reaches the southern door of the inner sanctum. Temple attendants get busy stretching a cordon to keep off crowd who push and crane their necks to get a sight of the image which is now being decorated for the *Arati*. We wait, sweating, acutely conscious of the audacious incongruity of the camera.

The time arrives. We hold our breath. The great chant begins. In the deafening crescendo I can just hear myself shouting 'start' and 'cut'.

The *Arati* goes on for an hour. The end finds us—and our raw stock—exhausted. As we are about to pack up, word arrives from the Mohant that he would like to hear the sound we have recorded. Would we be good enough to have our equipment conveyed to his apartment and the sound played back to him?

It takes half an hour to reach the Mohant's place with the equipment, another half to install it, and a full hour to play back and pack up. When we finally take leave of the great man it is a quarter to eleven. He smiles his approval. I almost expect him to tip us. . . .

1957

A Long Time on the Little Road ✐

I remember the first day's shooting of *Pather Panchali* very
well. It was in the festive season, in October, and the last
of the big *pujas* was taking place that day. Our location
was seventy-five miles away from Calcutta. As our taxi
sped along the Grand Trunk Road, we passed through
several suburban towns and villages and heard the drums
and even had fleeting glimpses of some images. Someone
said it would bring us luck. I had my doubts, but I wished
to believe it. All who set about making films need luck
as much as they need the other things: talent, money,
perseverance and so on. We needed a little more of it
than most.

I knew this first day was really a sort of rehearsal for us,
to break us in, as it were. For most of us it was a start from
scratch. There were eight on our unit of whom only one—
Bansi, the art director—had previous professional experience. We had a new cameraman, Subroto, and an old,
much-used Wall camera which happened to be the only
one available for hire on that particular day. Its one discernible advantage seemed to be a device to ensure smoothness of panning. We had no sound equipment, as the scene
was to be a silent one.

It was an episode in the screenplay where the two children
of the story, brother and sister, stray from their village
and chance upon a field of *kaash* flowers. The two have

had a quarrel, and here in this enchanted setting they are reconciled and their long journey is rewarded by their first sight of a railway train. I chose to begin with this scene because on paper it seemed both effective and simple. I considered this important, because the whole idea behind launching the production with only 8,000 rupees in the bank was to produce quickly and cheaply a reasonable length of rough cut which we hoped would establish our bonafides, the lack of which had so far stood in the way of our getting a financier.

At the end of the first day's shooting we had eight shots. The children behaved naturally, which was a bit of luck because I had not tested them. As for myself, I remember feeling a bit strung up in the beginning; but as work progressed my nerves relaxed and in the end I even felt a kind of elation. However, the scene was only half finished, and on the following Sunday we were back on the same location. But was it the same location? It was hard to believe it. What was on the previous occasion a sea of fluffy whiteness was now a mere expanse of uninspiring brownish grass. We knew *kaash* was a seasonal flower, but surely they were not that short-lived? A local peasant provided the explanation. The flowers, he said, were food to the cattle. The cows and buffaloes had come to graze the day before and had literally chewed up the scenery.

This was a big setback. We knew of no other *kaash* field that would provide the long shots that I needed. This meant staging the action in a different setting, and the very thought was heart-breaking. Who would have known then that we would be back on the identical location exactly two years later and indulge in the luxury of reshooting the entire scene with the same cast and the same unit but with money provided by the Government of West Bengal.

When I look back on the making of *Pather Panchali*,
I cannot be sure whether it has meant more pain to me
than pleasure. It is difficult to describe the peculiar tor-
ments of a production held up for lack of funds. The long
periods of enforced idleness (there were two gaps total-
ling a year and a half) produce nothing but the deepest
gloom. The very sight of the scenario is sickening, let alone
thoughts of embellishing it with details, or brushing up
the dialogue.

But work—even a day's work—has rewards, not the
least of which is the gradual comprehension of the complex and fascinating nature of film making itself. The edicts
of the theorists learnt assiduously over the years doubtless
perform some useful function at the back of your mind,
but grappling with the medium in a practical way for the
first time, you realise (*a*) that you know rather less about
it than you thought you did; (*b*) that the theorists do not
provide all the answers, and (*c*) that your approach should
derive not from Dovzhenko's *Earth*, however much you
may love that dance in the moonlight, but from the earth,
the soil, of your own country—assuming, of course, that
your story has its roots in it.

Bibhutibhusan Banerji's *Pather Panchali* was serialised
in a popular Bengali magazine in the early 1930s. The
author had been brought up in a village and the book
contained much that was autobiographical. The manus-
cript had been turned down by the publishers on the ground
that it lacked a story. The magazine, too, was initially
reluctant to accept it, but later did so on condition that
it would be discontinued if the readers so wished. But the
story of Apu and Durga was a hit from the first instalment.
The book, published a year or so later, was an outstanding critical and popular success and has remained on the
best-seller list ever since.

I chose *Pather Panchali* for the qualities that made it a great book: its humanism, its lyricism, and its ring of truth. I knew I would have to do a lot of pruning and reshaping—I certainly could not go beyond the first half, which ended with the family's departure for Banaras—but at the same time I felt that to cast the thing into a mould of cut-and-dried narrative would be wrong. The script had to retain some of the rambling quality of the novel because that in itself contained a clue to the feel of authenticity: life in a poor Bengali village does ramble.

Considerations of form, rhythm or movement did not worry me much at this stage. I had my nucleus: the family, consisting of husband and wife, the two children, and the old aunt. The characters had been so conceived by the author that there was a constant and subtle interplay between them. I had my time span of one year. I had my contrasts—pictorial as well as emotional: the rich and the poor, the laughter and the tears, the beauty of the countryside and the grimness of poverty existing in it. Finally, I had the two natural halves of the story culminating in two poignant deaths. What more could a scenarist want?

What I lacked was firsthand acquaintance with the *milieu* of the story. I could, of course, draw upon the book itself, which was a kind of encyclopaedia of Bengali rural life, but I knew that this was not enough. In any case, one had only to drive six miles out of the city to get to the heart of the authentic village.

While far from being an adventure in the physical sense, these explorations into the village nevertheless opened up a new and fascinating world. To one born and bred in the city, it had a new flavour, a new texture: you wanted to observe and probe, to catch the revealing details, the telling gestures, the particular turns of speech. You wanted to fathom the mysteries of 'atmosphere'. Does it consist in the

sights, or in the sounds? How to catch the subtle difference
between dawn and dusk, or convey the grey humid stillness
that precedes the first monsoon shower? Is sunlight in spring
the same as sunlight in autumn? . . .

The more you probed the more was revealed, and familiarity bred not contempt but love, understanding, tole-
rance. Problems of film making began to recede into the
background and you found yourself belittling the importance of the camera. After all, you said, it is only a recording
instrument. The important thing is Truth. Get at it and
you've got your great humanist masterpiece.

But how wrong you were! The moment you are on the
set the three-legged instrument takes charge. Problems
come thick and fast. Where to place the camera? High or
low? Near or far? On the dolly or on the ground? Is the
thirty-five O.K. or would you rather move back and use
the fifty? Get too close to the action and the emotion of
the scene spills over; get too far back and the thing becomes
cold and remote. To each problem that arises you must find
a quick answer. If you delay, the sun shifts and makes nonsense of your light continuity.

Sound is a problem too. Dialogue has been reduced to a
minimum, but you want to cut down further. Are those
three words really necessary, or can you find a telling gesture to take their place? The critics may well talk of a
laudable attempt at a rediscovery of the fundamentals of
silent cinema, but you know within your heart that while
there may be some truth in that, equally true was your
anxiety to avoid the uninspiring business of dubbing and
save on the cost of sound film.

Cost, indeed, was a dominant factor at all times, influenc-
ing the very style of the film. Another important factor—
and I would not want to generalise on this—was the human
one. In handling my actors I found it impossible to get to

the stage of impersonal detachment where I could equate them with so much raw material to be moulded and re-moulded at will. How can you make a woman of eighty stand in the hot midday sun and go through the same speech and the same actions over and over again while you stand by and watch with half-closed eyes and wait for that precise gesture and tone of voice that will mean perfection for you? This meant, inevitably, fewer rehearsals and fewer takes.

Sometimes you are lucky and everything goes right in the first take. Sometimes it does not and you feel you will never get what you are aiming at. The number of takes increases, the cost goes up, the qualms of conscience become stronger than the urge for perfection and you give up, hoping that the critics will forgive and the audience will overlook. You even wonder whether perhaps you were not being too finicky and the thing was not as bad or as wrong as you thought it was.

And so on and on it goes, this preposterous balancing act, and you keep hoping that out of all this will somehow emerge Art. At times when the strain is too much you want to give up. You feel it is going to kill you, or at least kill the artist in you. But you carry on, mainly because so much and so many are involved, and the day comes when the last shot is in the can and you are surprised to find yourself feeling not happy and relieved, but sad. And you are not alone in this. Everybody, from 'Auntie', for whom it has been an exciting if strenuous come-back after thirty years of oblivion, down to the little urchin who brought the live spiders and the dead toad, shares this feeling.

To me it is the inexorable rhythm of its creative process that makes film making so exciting in spite of the hardships and the frustrations. Consider this process: you have conceived a scene, any scene. Take the one where a young

girl, frail of body but full of some elemental zest, gives
herself up to the first monsoon shower. She dances in joy
while the big drops pelt her and drench her. The scene ex-
cites you not only for its visual possibilities but for its deeper
implications as well: that rain will be the cause of her
death.

You break down the scene into shots, make notes and
sketches. Then the time comes to bring the scene to life.
You go out into the open, scan the vista, choose your setting. The rain clouds approach. You set up your camera,
have a last quick rehearsal. Then the 'take'. But one is not
enough. This is a key scene. You must have another while
the shower lasts. The camera turns, and presently your
scene is on celluloid.

Off to the lab. You wait, sweating—this is September—
while the ghostly negative takes its own time to emerge.
There is no hurrying this process. Then the print, the
'rushes'. This looks good, you say to yourself. But wait.
This is only the content, in its bits and pieces, and not the
form. How is it going to join up? You grab your editor and
rush off to the cutting room. There is a gruelling couple of
hours, filled with aching suspense, while the patient process of cutting and joining goes on. At the end you watch
the thing on the moviola. Even the rickety old machine
cannot conceal the effectiveness of the scene. Does this
need music, or is the incidental sound enough? But that is
another stage in the creative process, and must wait until
all the shots have been joined up into scenes and all the
scenes into sequences and the film can be comprehended in
its totality. Then, and only then, can you tell—if you can
bring to bear on it that detachment and objectivity—if
your dance in the rain has really come off.

But is this detachment, this objectivity, possible? You
know you worked honestly and hard, and so did everybody

else. But you also know that you had to make changes, compromises—not without the best of reasons—on the set and in the cutting room. Is it better for them or worse? Is your own satisfaction the final test or must you bow to the verdict of the majority? You cannot be sure. But you can be sure of one thing: you are a better man for having made it.

1957

Problems of a Bengal Film Maker ✍

I suppose the only statement one can make about film making without fear of contradiction is that it is, at all times and all events, a complicated business. The cumbersomeness of its tools, the piecemeal nature of its creative process, the involvement of so many men and so much money, all combine to lend it an air of bizarre complexity.

The *avant-garde* experimentalist has to grapple with problems that are mainly of an aesthetic nature. He deals with them in much the same way as a painter or composer deals with problems of tone and texture and form. He is essentially a free artist, being responsible only to his own artistic conscience.

Far more complicated, to my mind, are the problems that beset the serious commercial film maker, for it is he who strives to turn an ostensible business enterprise into a stimulating creative pursuit and make the best of both art and commerce.

The problems that he faces in the process are extremely varied. Some are of a universal nature; others relate to conditions obtaining in his country, and yet others to the particular film he is making. But, whatever their nature, they all affect, in varying degrees, the final shape and quality of his film.

Working in India, and more specifically in Bengal, I have my own artistic problems as well as those that arise out of the peculiar circumstances of film making in my province, which is one of the three provinces where films are produced in India, the other two being Bombay and Madras.

We make films in the Bengali language. In Bombay, the language employed is Hindi, while in Madras it is Hindi as well as a choice of five different South Indian languages. Bengali is understood by about fifteen per cent of India's total population, which makes the market for Bengali films a very small one indeed. It has been calculated that if a Bengali film costs above Rs. 150,000 (£10,000), in nine cases out of ten it will not get its money back. A Hindi film can afford to spend six times as much and reasonably expect to make a profit.

As a result of this, investment in films in Bengal has been cautious and limited, and little has been done in the past twenty years or so in the way of technical improvements. Studios remain only partially equipped, laboratory work continues to be erratic, and a general air of privation pervades all departments of production. What Bengal has achieved so far has been more through human ingenuity and hard work than any skilled employment of technical resources.

Of the total number that constitutes the film-going public in our province, about twenty per cent is literate. Renoir once remarked that it was the alertness and receptivity of the French public that made possible the resurgence of the French cinema in the 'thirties'. The public that would support a truly serious film venture in Bengal is so small that it makes nothing longer than a two-reeler a safe business proposition. If one makes films aimed solely at this minority, one obviously makes them for love. In reality, no director can afford to do this, for once the stigma of esotericism attaches to his name, his days in the profession are numbered. Obviously, if he has to continue to earn his bread, he has to try and reach the larger suburban audience.

There are three familiar and well-trodden paths open to him. He can make mythological films, or he can make 'devotional' ones, or he can make 'socials'—preferably melodramas—which must have the adornment of the latest favourite star team. All three must have the usual concomitant of songs and dances and must not be below two and a half hours in length. This last proviso is so rigid, and so firm is the Exhibitor's faith in it, that a film which dares to disregard it may never see the light of day.

Needless to say, these formulas do not work every time, but they are the ones that have had the longest and the most lucrative existence. They have evolved out of the producers' deliberate and sustained playing down to a vast body of unsophisticated audience brought up on the simple tradition of the *Jatra*, a form of rural drama whose broad gestures, loud rhetoric and simple emotional patterns have been retained in the films to a degree unimaginable to those not familiar with this unique form of film making. The songs and dances too are a legacy of the theatrical-operatic tradition.

One can imagine a utopian situation when the spread of literacy might have gone hand in hand with an attempt on the part of the producers to come out of the groove and present the film-going public with something more worthwhile than tired reworking of hackneyed old patterns. But this has not happened, and is not likely to happen for some decades yet, unless some chance revolution should bring about the process. So the mythologicals and devotionals will stay and continue to provide the staple fare for the majority of Bengal's film public. What, then, should the serious film maker do? Should he accept the situation and apply himself to the making of *serious* mythologicals and *serious* devotionals, keeping the popular ingredients and clothing them in the semblance of art? This is obviously a way out of the impasse, but it raises an important question: can a serious film maker, working in India, afford to shut his eyes to the reality around him, the reality that is so poignant, and so urgently in need of interpretation in terms of the cinema? I do not think so.

For the truly serious, socially conscious film maker, there can be no prolonged withdrawal into fantasy. He must face the challenge of contemporary reality, examine the facts, probe them, sift them and select from them the material to be transformed into the stuff of cinema.

I say this with all conviction because I myself have been, in my own humble way, trying to do this, and have found out that sometimes it even pays to be uncompromising, and at all times, it makes one feel better to be so. Let me briefly recount my experience with my first two films.

When I began *Pather Panchali* in 1952, I was aware of the consequences of departing from the beaten track: past experience of other directors had warned me. But I was undeterred because I had great faith in my story, in its seemingly artless simplicity and in the appeal of its very recognisable, human characters. I also felt that if the departure were artistic enough, it would perhaps acquire the value of novelty which in itself would act as a bait to the public.

When the film was half finished and our money ran out, I was obliged to show the 5,000 ft. rough cut out to nearly every distributor in the province. They were unanimous in their distrust of the material. But this did not shake my faith in the story, and it was at last justified when the film was completed and released under government sponsorship. *Pather Panchali* was a hit in the cities. In the suburbs too it did unexpectedly well.

4

With the second film I grew bolder, and the consequences were less happy. My mistake, from a commercial point of view, was to take even bigger liberties with my source material than in *Pather Panchali*, which had at least retained the main contours of the original. As a result, the urban audience which was largely familiar with the plot of *Aparajito* was irritated by the deviations. As for the suburban audience, it was shocked by the portrayal of the mother and son relationship, so sharply at variance with the conventional notion of mutual sweetness and devotion.

Aparajito lost money. It was at this point that the European film festivals came into the picture. The awards won by the two films put a new complexion on the situation, and I realised that a Bengali film maker did not have to depend on the home market alone.

The situation that faces us now is this: working in Bengal, we are obliged morally and artistically to make films that have their roots in the soil of our province. Secondly, having in mind the nature of our audience and the resources at our disposal, we are further obliged to aim at an overall simplicity of approach. 'Big' stories are out, and so are big stars. The problem of reaching the masses cannot be solved yet, and will remain with us as long as illiteracy on a large scale exists. If the simple-but-serious approach can develop into a movement instead of being confined to a handful of individual directors, there is the possibility that the taste of the public can be moulded to accept the new and reject the old.

As for the audience abroad, they seem the likeliest to solve the financial problem, but our approach must be cautious and honest. There is no reason why we should not cash in on the foreigner's curiosity about the Orient. But this must not mean pandering to their love of the false-exotic. A great many notions about our country and our people have to be dispelled, even though it may be easier and—from a film point of view—more paying to sustain existing myths than to demolish them.

We expect no quick returns. Personally I have been lucky with my first two films, but what is really important and exciting is not the immediate gain, but the ultimate vindication of the belief that I hold dearest as an artist: art wedded to truth must in the end have its reward.

1958

Winding Route to a Music Room 🖋

'But have you been to Nimtita? Have you seen the palace there?' asked the old man in the teashop with the thatched roof. We were in the village of Lalgola, 150 miles from Calcutta, and we had just seen and rejected as unsuitable our thirtieth nobleman's palace.

'Nimtita? Where is that?' we asked without much enthusiasm. We had never heard of the place. 'It is sixty miles to the north of here. You drive up the highway. Then you come to a river and you cross it. A ferry will take your car across. Then up the highway again for twenty miles. Then a sign tells you where to branch off... It's on the river Padma, on the eastern bank. On the west is Pakistan. It's the palace of the Choudhurys. I've been listening to your talk, and I feel you ought to see this one before you give up.'

We were pretty sceptical of advice gratis from people who could not possibly have any conception of our needs. Anyway, the question was: do we or do we not undertake this one last exploration? If we did not like the palace, it might mean either abandoning the project, or seriously compromising it. A toss of the coin decided the issue, and we set out on our sixty-mile journey.

I was in bed with my right leg in plaster when I decided to film Tarasankar Banerji's famous short story, 'The Music Room' ('Jalsaghar'). A nasty fall on the stone steps at

Banaras had brought about a serious knee ailment. I lay
in bed and read all the Bengali books I could lay my hands
on. My standing with the distributors was not particularly
high at this point, and maybe this was one of the factors
which subconsciously influenced my choice of *The Music
Room*.

Here was a dramatic story which could be laced legiti-
mately with music and dancing, and distributors loved music
and dancing. But here, too, was scope for mood, for atmosphere, for psychological exploration. I decided on *The
Music Room* with a clear artistic conscience. I would cast
Chhabi Biswas, our greatest actor, in the leading role of the
zemindar (landowning nobleman) whose passion for staging lavish musical entertainments brings about his ruin.
But the crucial thing was to find a palace. As we had per-
force to have a low budget there was no question of indulg-
ing in the luxury of studio-built sets. I knew that given the
circumstances, my art director could be trusted to repro-
duce the architectural style and simulate the decay. But we
just didn't have the money for it.

Nimtita turned out to be everything that the old man
had claimed—and more. No one could have described in
words the feeling of utter desolation that surrounded the
palace. The Padma had changed its course over the years
so that now there were endless stretches of sandy waste where
once had been villages. The palace itself—Greek pillars,
entablature and all—was a perfect materialisation of my
dream image. It stood looking out over the desolation with
a worn and tragic dignity. It had miraculously escaped utter
obliteration through a whim of the river, which had approached within ten yards of the facade—having engulfed
the garden and the stables—and then stopped. Ganendra

Narayan Choudhury, who is seventy and owns a British title
and the palace, recalled the incident for us: 'We were having
breakfast one morning when we heard a low rumble. We
went out on the veranda and saw a sizable chunk of our
estate—almost a square mile of it—go under water, vanish-
ing forever. It all happened in a matter of seconds. Padma's
appetite is legendary.'

'But aren't you afraid that the river might encroach
further?'

'Oh yes, the rains bring with them the usual qualms.'

'Then why do you stay here?'

'We'd sooner go down with the house than desert it.'

The Nimtita palace was perfect, except that the music
room—it did have one, for Ganendra Narayan's uncle
Upendra Narayan Choudhury had been a patron of music
much like the nobleman in our story—was not impressive
enough to serve as the setting for the sumptuous soirées
that I had planned. This would have to be built in a match-
ing style in the studio. And there were two other essential elements of our story which Mr Choudhury lacked.
He did have an elephant twenty years ago, but not any
more; and he did not have a white stallion. The horse was
located in a private stable in Calcutta. It belonged to an
aristocrat who had seen better days, and was now finding
it difficult to maintain his brougham. He was glad to sell
the horse to us for 200 rupees. The elephant belonged
to a rajah who was persuaded to loan it to us. It travelled
a distance of 165 miles on foot to the location, crossing five
rivers on the way.

On returning from our first trip to Nimtita, I telephoned
the author, Mr Banerji. He had been just as anxious about
the location as we were.

'We've found our palace at last, Mr Banerji,' I said.

'Have you? And where is it?'

'At an obscure place called Nimtita.'

'Nimtita?' There was a note of recognition in his voice. 'You don't mean the palace of the Choudhurys, do you?'

'That's the one.'

'But that's extraordinary! I haven't been to Nimtita myself, but I've read about the Choudhurys in a history of Bengal zemindars, and it was the music-loving Upendra Narayan Choudhury who served as the model for my rajah.'

1963

Film Making

Of the many questions that I have been asked by interviewers over the last ten years or so, two have recurred more frequently than any others. The first is: 'How and why did you come into films?' This has generally been asked in the knowledge that I had started my career in advertising, as a graphic designer. To the questioner, the transition probably seemed too abrupt, too arbitrary. How does one design soap wrappings one day and shape the contours of a celluloid saga the next?

In my answer, I have usually managed to sustain the mystery with a nodding smile that suggests a secret metamorphosis, a sort of occult elevation to a higher status of creativity. As a matter of fact, my own conviction is that as a transition from one field of creative activity to another, this is not really such a rough one. After all, both films and advertising deal with consumable commodities and in both you have the spectacle of the conscientious artist striving to express himself in aesthetic terms; while the sponsor, hovering in the background and caring little for Art, concerns himself solely with profits. Somebody—I do not remember who—has defined the Cinema as the highest form of commercial art. After ten years in this profession, I have no quarrel with that definition.

Was I conscious of this aspect when I first made my transition from a safe desk job to the uncertainties of shooting a projected epic in the unglamorous backwoods of a Bengali village? I often put myself this question, trying to locate the mainsprings of an adventure that was, to say the least, hazardous.

I know one thing for certain; and that is, I had no intention of making an esoteric film. I knew what I was going to do was off-beat, but I never equated novelty with risk. If anything, I had the opposite conviction. I knew also that I had a basically good 'property', as they say, in *Pather Panchali*. It was a well-loved story and one that was widely read and praised. But the film industry in Bengal at that time was geared to the so-called 'safe' conventional approach and nobody had ever heard of a film being made by somebody who had not spent at least six years mooching around in a film studio in some capacity or other.

The usual credentials for a director making a film for the first time would be either to have served a longish term as a first assistant to a director, or to have been a cameraman, or, at least, a writer of film scripts. I had been none of these things. What I did have was long years of looking at films—firstly, in my school days, as a film fan, and later as a serious student of the cinema, reading about techniques and taking hieroglyphic notes in the darkness of an auditorium. These notes concerned cutting methods of various directors—mostly American—such as Ford, Capra, Huston, Wyler and Wilder.

Coexisting with this admiration for the best of Hollywood was a growing despair with the uncinematic methods displayed in the home-grown product. This latter feeling, may I add, only helped to fan my enthusiasm. I could not believe that an amateur with the right ideas—if given the chance—could do worse than professionals who started out on the wrong foot. Lest I sound too critical of the Bengali cinema of the fifties, I should like to add that it had its admirable aspects too—some good acting, some imaginative photography, stretches of well-planned and well-cut scenes here and there, and, almost invariably, some good, believable dialogue. But never the feeling of satisfactory total achievement.

The main weakness was a formal one, and about this I have a little theory of my own. Indian directors tended to overlook the musical aspect of a film's structure.

The reason lies surely in the absence of a dramatic narrative tradition in Indian music. It is valid to speak of a Beethoven symphony in terms of universal brotherhood, or man's struggle against fate or the passionate outpourings of a soul in torment. Western classical music underwent a process of humanisation with the invention of the sonata form—with its masculine first subjects and feminine second subjects and their interweaving and progress through a series of dramatic key-changes, to a point of culmination.

But a *raga* is a *raga*—with a single predetermined mood and tonality—that is, built up like a temple, starting from a solid base of *alap*, culminating in a spire of flourishes on the higher octaves of the scale. Perhaps one could, with some stretch of imagination, think of a film subject that might be built up like the development of a *raga*, but I cannot think of this as a form with wide application. At any rate, the vast majority of stories that provide the material for our films can only be told in a style that has already found universal application—in the style which originated in Hollywood.

The sense of form, of a rhythmic pattern existing in time, is what was mainly lacking in our directors. This meant in effect a lack of good scenario writers—for the broader aspects of a film's rhythm are already contained in the scenario. All the refinements of mood, tonality, texture and so on are provided by the various elements that come into play at the stage of execution.

Although I was convinced that I was armed with a formidable array of theoretical knowledge, film making seemed a terribly hard job in the beginning. On the very first day of the shooting of *Pather Panchali*, I remember I had a scene where the boy Apu went looking for his sister into a field of tall grass. In the very first shot all that the boy had to do was to walk a few steps, stop, look this way and that, and then walk again. Little did I know then that it was twice as hard to achieve impeccability in a shot like that than in a shot of, say, a charging cavalry. With the latter, all you need is a cavalry that charges. In Hollywood, such a shot, or even an entire scene of battle, would normally be entrusted to what is known as the second-unit director—a sturdy young fellow, generally, with not much brains but a lot of stamina. William Wyler was away planning interiors in Hollywood while the second-unit director shot the entire chariot race somewhere in Italy. But if you are faced with a scene of a boy looking for his sister in a field of tall grass, you are faced with a particular state of mind that produces a special kind of walk, and a special kind of stopping and turning of the head. You also have to calculate the exact duration of the halt, the exact duration of each turn of head, the exact moment of the resumption of walk. Of course, all this is further complicated if you are dealing with someone who has never faced a camera before, and with whom it would be futile to discuss outer manifestations of inner feelings.

If this first shot pulled me up and taught me a lesson, it was also an eye-opener. It revealed to me the most chal-

lenging aspect of film making, which is the exploration
of the truth of human behaviour and the revelation of that
truth through the medium of actors. Experience tells us that
the subtlest of emotional states affects a person's speech and
behaviour and such revealing speech and behaviour is at
the very heart of cinema's eloquence.

I like to think that it was a shrewd move on my part
to have selected for my first film a story where one had
to put the emphasis on the human aspect. Not only was
this wise from the box office point of view, but with the
means at our disposal, any preoccupation with technique
would have been disastrous.

But balancing of means and ends is not an easy process,
and a certain impatience sometimes makes a director
plunge into a subject that is clearly beyond his scope. Such
was the case with *The Music Room*, my third film.

I was by then a little tired of the rural scene, so I decided
to film this story of decadent feudalism. For the exteriors
for this story, we needed a crumbling nineteenth century
nobleman's palace, and found a magnificent one in Murshi-
dabad, right on the bank of the river Padma. But there
was also a lot of studio interiors to do, and little did we
realise that the place where we had committed ourselves
to shoot them was also in a state of abject decay. As a
result we constantly found ourselves in the position of
wanting to do things for which the means were just not
there. The music room itself, where the nobleman held his
soirées, was the largest set we had ever built, and having
built it, we found that it called for overhead shots from a
crane.

The studio did not have a crane. I had just won an
award at Cannes and felt justified in asking for a crane to
be fetched from a bigger studio at the other end of the
city. The enormous hunk of a contraption arrived on top

of a truck. We were told we could keep it for a week. At
the end of the week, having taken the shots I needed, I
asked for the crane to be sent back.

The truck arrived in the evening. In the failing light
I watched the crane being pushed along a couple of stout
wooden planks on to the top of the truck. It seemed a
risky operation. And then, before I realised what was happening, half way up the plank, the crane tottered for an
instant and then crashed on the coolies, killing one instantly and crippling another for life. I stood rooted to
the spot, barely ten feet away, stunned by the magnitude
and suddenness of the tragedy. It took me some time to
realise that all this would not have happened if I had not
set my mind on those overhead shots.

The striving to find a balance between means and ends
applies particularly to a place like Bengal where the small-
ness of the market and the circumstances of distribution
provide an automatic check on technical expansion. For
instance, when in 1962 I decided to make a film in colour,
I had to plan the whole thing in terms of shooting on location, because it is not worthwhile for studios here to em-
ploy the number of lights needed for shooting interiors. If
I wanted to shoot a colour film in a studio, I would probably have to do it in Bombay and Madras. The cost would
be too high for a Bengali film, and one would have to think
in terms of Hindi or Tamil. Since I believe it is impossible
to make a good film in a language one is not fluent in, I
see little chance of that happening. It is as simple as that,
really.

Talking of means and ends, I think the primary reason
why the New Wave films have that rough edge to them is
that they cannot afford the polish. Polish is really a matter

of time, and in films, as we all learn sooner or later, time equates perfectly with money. With true Gallic flair, the New Wave has turned this lack into a virtue. They have done away with both conventional story and conventional style. If *Jules et Jim* set out to tell a conventional story, one would be merely irritated by the jump-cuts and freeze-frames and hand-held shots that jag its contours. Truffaut is far too sensible an artist to do that. We may not identify or sympathise with the droll waywardness of its characters, but there is no denying its stylistic consistency and therefore its validity as a work of art.

Of the other major European film makers, Antonioni displays a rare economy of means. At heart he is a classicist; the structure of his stories reveals that. On the surface his films are stark and devoid of frills. Feelings are muted, and there is a genuine attempt at a revelation of states of mind through action and behaviour. Antonioni's films stand or fall on the degree of conviction achieved in their human relationship.

Fellini from the same country is a romantic and at the other extreme from Antonioni. I am eclectic enough to be able to admire both, although I feel that with his wider sympathies, his wit and his greater vitality and optimism Fellini will have a longer creative life than Antonioni.

This brings me to the second question that the interviewers like to put me, and that is: 'Who has influenced you most in your work?'

Ten years ago, my stock answer to this was a series of three or four names that I felt the questioner was anticipating. Flaherty, and Renoir and Donskoi. Flaherty because he made films about rural folk, Renoir because he was a humanist, and had made *The River* in Calcutta two years before I started *Pather Panchali*, and Donskoi because he had made the Gorki films—so similar in their

ingredients to *Pather Panchali*. After a time, I got a little
tired of the knowing nod that greeted my answer. Of late,
I have started to name classical Sanskrit dramatists and
eighteenth century German composers. Sometimes, for a
change, I mention the author of the book on which the
film under discussion is based as the dominant source.

Now all these answers are partially true. No film maker,
working in the advanced stage of the cinema's development, can deny that he has learned from past masters, or
even present ones. But what one really absorbs from other
film makers are the externals of technique. The lighting of
a particular close-up that sticks in the mind, the placing of
the camera for a particular grouping, cutting back and
forth from face to face in a scene of dialogue—all these
one may notice and store up at the back of one's mind—
just as a writer would note a striking turn of phrase in
another writer. But what one notes and admires particularly in a director is his attitude—the reflection of the
man himself and his sympathies—which puts a distinctive
stamp on his work, on his chosen theme as well as on the
manner of its unfolding. Here let me digress and relate an
incident.

In 1958, I was invited to attend a film seminar at the
Flahertys' place in Vermont in the United States. Mrs
Flaherty had read somewhere of her husband's influence
on my work and was already an admirer of *Pather Panchali*.
She told me that the film had the unmistakable ring of truth
in it and then asked me how I had handled the people—the
children, the old auntie and so forth, and whether I faced
the same problems as her husband did. It was not easy
to bring myself to break her illusion, but I did it. I told
her that none of the main actors came from that village

or from any village for that matter. The children were studying in a school in Calcutta, the mother had a Master of Arts degree and the old auntie had been on the professional stage.

It took me quite a while to convince Mrs Flaherty that in films it was the end result that mattered and the fact that the characters were faked implied no lack of sympathy for the people portrayed.

Ten years of film making has taught me, above anything else, not to make a fetish of anything. I enjoy working with non-actors, but I also enjoy putting professionals and non-pros together and watch the non-pros acquire confidence from the professionals and professionals benefit from the artless simplicity of the non-pros.

I like working on locations—even interiors. But I know now that with an imaginative art director and an observant cameraman it is possible to fake interiors so that the shrewdest professional eye is fooled.

Once in a while I feel like having a fling at a hand-held freeze-frame, jump-cut New Wave venture; but one thing stops me short here: I know I cannot have thàt bedroom scene that goes with it.

1965

The Odds against Us

Although the precise involvements of a film maker are not widely publicised, there is a general, if vague, awareness that film making is a tough business. There are some films —the big Hollywood 'blockbusters', for instance—which wear this toughness on their sleeves as it were. Battles, orgies, earthquakes, conflagrations, triumphal processions —who needs to be told that you cannot get these by a snap of your fingers? With the backing of money, men and materials, it is easy for Hollywood to make a *Spartacus*, or for Soviet Russia to make a *War and Peace*. In Madrid, they will show you the cities of Rome and Moscow and Peking which were built for costly co-productions and left standing as tourist attractions.

Here in India, and more particularly in Bengal, we dare not plunge into epics as vast as these. For one thing, we do not have the money. Even if we did have the money, we would not have the market, and certainly not the know-how to compete with Hollywood. That is why—and not because we do not have the predilection—we have chosen for ourselves the field of the intimate cinema: the cinema of mood and atmosphere rather than of grandeur and spectacle. It is amusing to reflect that the favourite publicity catchline of the blockbusters—'two years in the making' —might equally well have been applied to the first such 'intimate' film that I made: *Pather Panchali*. But here the

phrase would have had the cadence of a dirge, and not a
fanfare; because for long stretches we just sat idle for lack
of funds, and what money we received came in small
trickles.

Speaking of myself, as far as financial backing is concerned, things are not as bad as they used to be when I
started out. Does this suggest that now I have a cushy job
making films rather than a tough one? Not by a long shot.
We here are beset with a very special set of problems, indigenous to the place and arising out of the special codes that
guide our lives and shape our destinies.

Let us begin at the beginning. How do we get about
making a film? What is the first step? To find a story, of
course: a 'property', as they say. Now, assuming that the
choice is made by the director, which is as it should be,
and also assuming that he has not taken up the profession merely to fool about with a chancy medium in the
hope of making some quick money—we can be certain
that his choice is based on two major considerations:
(*a*) his affinity with the theme of the story, and (*b*) his
belief that the story would make a good film. If the director is not a greenhorn, he will also have taken into account
his public. Experience has taught him that this would be
for his own good. If his film did not bring back its cost, his
backers would lose faith in him. And when one backer loses
faith in a director, other backers tend to follow suit, as a
result of which in no time the director finds himself branded
as a bad risk. So the wise director learns to lower his brow
a little. It means that he cannot operate on the level of
a fashionable aesthete like, say, Alain Resnais. *Avant-gardism*
is a luxury which we cannot yet afford in our country.
What we can do—and do profitably—is to explore new
themes, new aspects of society, new facets of human relationships. But if you want to do that, and be serious and

,artistic about it, you cannot afford to sugar your pill for the masses who are used to tasty morsels of make-believe. You have to be content with a minority public; which in turn means that you have to have a tight rein on your budget.

Balancing the budget, tricky as it is, is unfortunately not the only problem that the serious film maker faces. In the choice of story itself, he is faced with limiting factors nonexistent in other countries. For instance, a full-bodied treatment of a story of physical passion—and such stories, great ones even, are not lacking in our literature—is unthinkable on the Indian screen. I used a shot of a couple kissing in *Devi*, but did not venture beyond a long shot with the lovers silhouetted behind a mosquito netting. I am sure if I had gone in for a close-up and lit the action more clearly, catcalls from the lower stalls would have ruined my delicate mood-setting sound track of shrilling crickets and distant howling jackals. The scenes of lovemaking in Indian films have therefore been reduced to a formula of clasping hands, longing looks, and vapid, supposedly amorous verbal exchanges—not to speak of love duets sung against artificial romantic backdrops. It is the dead-weight of ultra-Victorian moral conventions which reduces the best of directors to taking refuge in these devices. Speaking of myself, I would in the circumstances prevailing sooner discard a story, however good, that called for an open treatment of the love aspect than ruin it by dilution.

Let us now see how far we can go with a political theme here. Can we make an *Advice and Consent*? A *Dr. Strangelove*? A *Judgment at Nuremberg*? I think not. Can we show a corrupt Congressman? I should like to try and find out, but my guess is that we cannot. Can we show a poor bank clerk getting rich by dubious means and wearing a

Gandhi cap to hide his baldness? We can, but we may be
asked, as I was, by the Board of Censors, to paint the cap
black on the celluloid. If you want to show an office boss
to be small-minded by having him make snide remarks
about an Anglo-Indian employee whom you have portrayed in a sympathetic way, you may be thought of as
sharing the boss's prejudices. And this will be held against
you in Delhi when your film comes up for an official prize.
And heaven help you if you take up a classic and deviate
even the tiniest bit from it, because then you will have a
host of 'intellectuals' turning at a moment's notice into a
horde of belligerent Tynans who will swoop down on you
and tear you limb from limb.

The upshot of all this is that, story-wise, you have to
operate within a somewhat narrow field, and some of your
cherished ambitions may have to wait until good sense
prevails amongst the powers that be.

Let us now assume that you have a good script that you
feel would make a good film, and that your backer also
feels is a worthwhile proposition. What next? Casting, of
course—the first step in the process of 'interpretation'.

Some of the roles are, of course, pre-cast. Even when you
had read the story, you could picture X as playing the husband, Y the wife and baby Z the cute little daughter. But
what about the doddering, toothless 80-year-old grandpa?
And what about all those bit parts that dot the story—
men, women, children, peasants, shopkeepers, professors,
prostitutes and so on and so on?

Almost anywhere else in the world you will find agents
who keep fat dossiers on available 'extras'. You only have
to turn the pages to pick your players. If you want 'un-
knowns', you put ads in the papers or set talent-scouts

scouting. We have no agents here, and no talent-scouts. You can put ads in the dailies, of course, but my own experience is that people with talent suffer from an inhibiting fear of rejection and never answer ads. What you usually get goes straight into the waste-paper basket.

So you are left to scour the streets and scan the faces of pedestrians. Or go to race-meets and cocktails and wedding receptions, all of which you hate from the bottom of your heart.

If you want Chinese extras (as I did, in *Aparajito*) for a shot that lasts a minute and a half, it may land you in a Chinese brothel, where you sit in the anteroom—dank and dark as a primordial cave—the smell of opium stifling your nostrils, while Madam saunters in and out showing her yellowing teeth in a smile of hopeful invitation. The promised extras take hours to show up, but you are stuck not just because there is blinding rain outside, but because you hope to get the shot as you planned it.

I have generally been lucky in finding the right players for my parts, but the possibility of failure is always around the corner. There is just now an alarming shortage of good professional actors and actresses of middle age and above. There are roles that can only be brought to life by professionals. *Pather Panchali* could never be made now because Chunibala is no longer there. *Jalsaghar*, *Devi*, *Kanchenjunga*, were all written with Chhabi Biswas in mind. Ever since he died, I have not written a single middle-aged part that calls for a high degree of professional talent.

Once the casting is done, I am ready to plunge headlong into the business of shooting. The studios in Calcutta show their hallowed past in every crevice on the wall, in every tatter on the canvas that covers the ceiling. Some of the families of rodents that inhabit the rafters have lived there ever since the foundation of the industry. The floor is pitted,

the camera groans as it turns, the voltage begins to drop
after sundown. The general air of shabbiness is unnerving.
And yet I do not mind these at all. I do not think of these
as hindrances. After all, we have the essentials to make a
film, and it is within us to make it badly or well. It is the
bareness of means that forces us to be economical and
inventive, and prevents us from turning craftsmanship into
an end in itself. And there is something about creating
beauty in the circumstances of shoddiness and privation that
is truly exciting.

Yes, I am happy to be working where I am.

1966

Some Aspects of My Craft ✍

Story and Script
I have so far made thirteen films of which eleven have been based on existing stories.

Of the Trilogy, *Pather Panchali* was followed by *Aparajito*, but two films intervened between *Aparajito* and *Apur Sansar*. When I started *Pather Panchali*, there was no thought of following it up with two other films on Apu. We could not look beyond one film at that stage. The success of *Pather Panchali* made possible the making of Part II.

After *Aparajito*, the main urge was to make something different—in style, mood and texture. Hence the satirical fantasy *Paras Pathar*. This was followed by another extreme contrast—*Jalsaghar*. Going back to Apu was easy after these two contrasted interludes.

I find I am inimical to the idea of making two similar films in succession. Twice I have felt bored with the long feature and have gone in for collections of short stories. There are certain things I would like to do—an epic, a historical, a science-fiction—which I cannot for want of backing.

I do not know if all this suggests a restlessness of mind, an indecision, a lack of direction, resulting in a blurring of outlook—or if there is an underlying something which binds my disparate works together. All I know is that I am interested in many aspects of life, many periods in history, many styles and many genres of film making, and I expect to keep shifting gears and venturing into new fields— thematically and stylistically.

When I write my own story, I use characters and milieus I am familiar with. I can deal with something I do not know at first hand only with the help of someone who does (Bibhutibhusan's village, Tarasankar's world of zemindars, Tagore's Renaissance Bengal).

When I am using someone else's story, it obviously means that I find some aspects of the story attractive for certain reasons. These aspects are always evident in the film. Others which I find unsatisfactory are either left out or modified to suit my needs. I do not give a thought to purists who rage at departure from the original.

In my own experience, I am happy to say, these purists have never included the authors of the original stories. Parasuram was living when I made a film of his ten-page short story *Paras Pathar*. He read the script and heartily approved of the liberties I had taken. The same applies to Premendra Mitra (*Kapurush*) and Narendra Mitra (*Mahanagar*). The critics made no comments on the changes in these stories, presumably because they were afraid the authors might take my side against them if they did. The main invectives, predictably enough, have been hurled against my Tagore adaptations.

I find I have lost my taste for 'Sagas', or for any extended novelistic subjects for that matter. I feel convinced that the long short story is ideally suited to the two-hour span of the normal commercial film.

When writing an original story, my predilection is for working densely within a restricted field in terms of time and space. Planning the story of *Nayak*, I dismissed quite early the notion of an orderly, step-by-step account of the making of a matinee idol. That seemed to belong to the cinema of the thirties and forties. In the film, the hero's part is revealed in flashbacks and dreams which make inroads into a very tight time-space pattern (twenty-four hours in a train).

Casting

Hollywood in its heyday used to buy properties and write stories to suit the talents of big money-making stars. One could say with a good deal of truth that the stars came before the stories.

This has been a common phenomenon in the performing arts for centuries. Mozart wrote important works for certain virtuosos. Ballets have been composed around gifted danseuses. In recent times, Benjamin Britten has been inspired to write a cello concerto for Rostropovich. So, too, in Hollywood and films. Stories for Garbo, Dietrich, Bogart, Brando, Marilyn Monroe. And was not Chaplin always looking for something for the Tramp to do? And in more recent times—what about Antonioni and Monica Vitti, Godard and Anna Karina, Fellini and Giulietta Massina? I doubt if *Wild Strawberries* would have been made if Bergman had not felt like paying homage to Victor Sjöström.

The Trilogy was one work of mine which was conceived entirely without reference to available acting material. As a result, most of the parts had to be filled by newcomers.

On the other hand, I wrote *Paras Pathar* with Tulsi Chakravarty in mind, *Nayak* was written for Uttam Kumar, *Kanchenjunga*, *Devi* and *Jalsaghar* for Chhabi Biswas.

Many stories never get beyond the stage of contemplation because they prove uncastable.

Handling Actors

I never rehearse except on a finished set. This means—
since we cannot afford to keep a set standing for too long
—that rehearsals have to be kept to a minimum.

I do not think it is important to discuss a part thoroughly
with an actor, but if he so wishes, I have no fetish against
obliging him.

When rehearsing, I usually give brief instructions to my
actors and ask them to act out a scene on that basis. They
inevitably colour it with their own ideas about the scene.
The combined effect of these two I use as raw material
on which I mould the performances.

Sometimes, with a minimum of guidance, an actor provides me with exactly what I want. Sometimes I have to try
and impose a precise manner, using the actor almost as a
puppet. This is my inevitable method with children.

Since it is the ultimate effect on the screen that matters,
any method that helps to achieve the desired effect is
valid.

Designing

Like everything else in film making, designing or art direction has two aspects to it: the craftsmanship and the aesthetics. The first belongs entirely in the domain of the designer.
The second has a direct bearing on the story and derives
from it.

The story indicates the period, the locale, the social status
of persons occupying certain habitats, the props which
serve important functions. The designer has to work within
the limits of these specifications. This is not necessarily a
constricting factor, but it does impose on him a collabora-
tive and interpretative function rather than an independent
creative one (exceptions are stories with stylised settings).

But even within such specifications, there is enough room for details which can enliven a setting. Often the use of imaginative props can suggest facets of a character not immediately revealed through speech and action. This is the area where a gifted designer can make his strongest contribution.

To the extent that a director knows what he wants, he can impose his ideas on the designer. The designer is independent only up to the point the director allows him.

Once a set has been built after the necessary collaboration between designer and director, the job of the designer ends and the director takes over, arranging and rearranging props, adding and subtracting details to suit the needs of a given scene, a given situation.

Simulated natural settings are obsolete now, and exteriors are shot on real locations. If one shoots interiors in actual settings, one achieves the quality of verisimilitude. But there are limiting factors such as poor sound recording (involving the always unsatisfactory business of dubbing), restricted camera movement, interference from onlookers, etc. By and large, I prefer to shoot interiors in the studio where with a gifted collaboration of my designer and my cameraman I can almost always achieve what I want.

Camera Work

Here art and aesthetics are not so easily separable from technique and craft. Use of particular lenses, particular film stocks, of diaphragms, filters, lights—these are all matters of technique related to the physical and chemical aspects of photography, as well as matters of aesthetics affecting the very mood and texture of a film.

The style of photography should grow out of the story, and the director should be aware of what he wants and

be able to convey it in precise terms to the cameraman.

Ideally, the director should be his own cameraman or
at least be able to impose a visual approach on his cameraman. Flaherty cranked his own camera on some of his
greatest films, and Orson Welles so assuredly set his own
stamp on the photography of his films that the work of
a veteran like Gregg Toland (*Citizen Kane*) became almost
indistinguishable from that of a comparative unknown like
Stanley Cortez (*Magnificent Ambersons*).

There is no such thing as good photography *per se*. It is
either right for a certain kind of film, and therefore good;
or wrong—however lush, well-composed, meticulous—and
therefore bad.

It is dangerous for a cameraman to put forward creative
suggestions unless he has the full emotional and visual
sweep of the film in his head. If he does not, he should
be content to do as the director tells him. Coutard is a good
cameraman if only because he is willing to sacrifice his ego
and submit to Godard, whose ideas, if unconventional, are
at all times striking, and therefore worthy of respect.

The role of a cameraman varies according to the director
he is working with. A director weak on the visual side may
be considerably helped by a cameraman with a sense of
drama. When a director is a true *auteur*—that is, if he
controls every aspect of production—then the cameraman
is obliged to perform an interpretative role. Whenever he
does more than that, the director should humbly part with
some of his credit as an *auteur*. Good sets, good equipment,
good film stock, good processing and printing—these are
all contributing factors in good photography. For certain
types of film, one does not need the best of everything.
For instance, the early De Sica films could be made and
in fact were made effectively with faulty indifferent tech-

nical equipment. But one could not imagine a Max Ophüls film with a harsh edge to it visually.

Conventional ideas about beautiful photography are fast dying, although some strange dicta still persist. One such is the careful lighting of the heroine's face at all times under all circumstances. This is considered a commercial necessity and some prima donnas of the screen are so pampered by this practice that they cannot stand a cameraman who does not know the 'angles' of their faces. Even the best cameramen sometimes yield to this for the sheer pleasure of lighting a well-modelled face, or for the challenge of beautifying an unbeautiful one. The cameraman who cannot curb his instincts to take a pretty shot is often acting against the best interests of the film.

Ever since *Charulata* I have been operating the camera myself. This is not because I do not trust my cameraman's operational abilities, but because I want to know exactly at all times how a shot is going, not only in terms of acting, but of acting viewed from a chosen set-up which imposes a particular spatial relationship between the actors. This relationship may keep changing in the shot through movement of the actors, or of the camera, or both. Through the lens is the only position from which these changes can be precisely gauged.

New lenses, new portable lighting equipment, new devices for tracking and panning—all these I feel are adding greatly to the expressive power of the cinema. The zoom is a remarkable invention—not just as a time-saving substitute for tracking, but in its own right for its power of varying the emphasis.

Subroto, my cameraman, has evolved, elaborated and perfected a system of diffused lighting whereby natural daylight can be simulated to a remarkable degree. This results in a photographic style which is truthful, unobtrusive and modern. I have no doubt that for films in the realistic genre, this is a most admirable system.

Editing

My editor Dulal and I edit the 'rushes' as we go along, taking time over it so that in the final cutting only the finest points need our attention.

Much of my cutting is done in the camera. That is to say, I shoot very little beyond the point where I know the cut will come. I make no special artistic claim for this but it does make for economy—a vital factor at all times with us in Bengal.

As a result of this the editor has to work a good bit of the time as a 'joiner', with only a limited creative contribution to make. But there are scenes where he really comes into his own. The most challenging are scenes of dialogue which involve cutting back and forth from speaker to speaker, from speech to reaction. This offers endless variations of emphasis, unlimited scope for pointing up shades of feeling. It is not unusual for an important dialogue scene to be cut in half a dozen different ways before a final satisfactory form is achieved.

The contribution that a creative editor makes to such a scene is a vital one, although the critic is more likely to overlook it and notice the more obvious and spectacular evidences of scissors at work.

Editing is the stage where a film really begins to come to life and one is never more aware of the uniqueness of the film medium than in watching a well-cut scene pulsate with a life of its own.

Music

Since *Teen Kanya* I have taken to composing the music for my own films. Before that I had worked with Ravi

Shankar (four times), Ali Akbar Khan and Vilayet Khan (once each). The reason why I do not work with professional composers any more is that I get too many musical ideas of my own, and composers, understandably enough, resent being guided too much.

I get my ideas fairly quickly—sometimes as early as in the scenario stage. I jot them down as they come. Usually they come clothed in a certain orchestral colour, and I make a note of that too. But the actual work of scoring has to wait until I am through with everything else, including final cutting.

Of all the stages of film making, I find it is the orchestration of the music that needs my greatest concentration. The task may be lightened when I have acquired more fluency in scoring. At the moment, it is still a painstaking process.

But the pleasure of finding out that the music sounds as you had imagined it would, more than compensates for the hard work that goes into it. The final pleasure, of course, is in finding out that it not only sounds right but is also right for the scene for which it was meant.

1966

Those Songs ✒

'Hindi films? You mean the ones with a lot of singing?' Yes, indeed. And the definition has spread further and wider than one would imagine. Abroad, I have often been asked—in a hesitant, tentative sort of way, as if the question might offend me—why this should be so. Actually there are several possible answers and I have tried them all at various times. There is the one about Indians being very *fond* of music. 'They love songs, you know. They keep going back just for the songs.' But this usually provokes a second question: are they fond of it to such an extent that you just cannot sell a film without songs? This is a stumping one because there is really no ethnic evidence that Indians are more fond of singing than, say, the Italians or the Spanish—or even the Russians and the Americans. A second answer goes well with a shrug. 'You know how it is . . . you have a film with a song that clicks . . . then you have another . . . then another . . .' and you let that trail off with a shrug. The gloomy hint in this one is unmistakable: the vitality of the medium is being inexorably sapped by this sprouting, spreading musical infection.

A third answer, perhaps the truest, is that to the vast conglomerate mass that makes up the Indian public the cinema is the only form of available inexpensive entertainment. They have not the choice that the western public has of music halls, revues, plays, concerts, and even, sometimes, of a permanent circus. Yet the craving for spectacle, for romance, for a funny turn or two, for singing and dancing, remains and has somehow to be met. If the film does not meet it, nothing else will.

So you have the circumstances and the basis for a formula and there is no denying that if you think in terms of tired untutored minds with undeveloped tastes needing an occasional escape through relaxation, you will have to admit that the best prescription is a well-mixed potpourri of popular entertainment. And that is exactly what is being contrived and will, I suspect, continue to be contrived for a very long time yet. The remarkable thing is that the practice is so old, so widespread and so ingrained that we tend to lose sight of the unique traits it has developed. It may be worthwhile to take a look at them, for they are the only things which remain immutable in the face of global upheavals in the cinema.

If I were asked to find room for six songs in a story that is not expressly a 'musical', I would have to throw up my hands and give up. If I were forced, I would either revolt or go berserk. And yet six songs per film, per *every* film, is the accepted average, and at no point in the history of Indian films has there been an uproar against it except from a tiny highbrow minority who write about it in snickering terms in the pages of little magazines whose readership would barely fill a decent-sized cinema. I once read a critique of a Hindi film in an American magazine which actually praised the use of songs as a sort of Brechtian alienation device, something which purposely makes the spectator aware of the artificiality of the whole thing. 'A very interesting piece of stylisation,' said the reviewer, 'wholly in the non-realistic tradition of Indian art.' I do not know if the film makers themselves think of the songs in these terms. Personally I would not mind the songs if they

6

did not go against the grain of a film. And from an aesthetic point of view, too, there would be nothing to object to
them if they did not.

Another strange practice that the public blandly accepts
is that whoever breaks into song in a film does so in the
voice of one of a half-a-dozen popular singers who seem
to have cornered the playback market. Once in a long
while, through sheer accident, the singing voice may match
with the speaking one, but it is never expected to. To one
not familiar with the practice the change of timbre usually
comes as a jolt. But for the audience here the jolt would
probably come if they did not recognise one of their six
favourites in the playback.

It is also surprising how much thought goes into the
cinematic handling ('picturisation', as the term goes) of
these song numbers. Yes, the songs too—not just the
dances. Dances are at any rate things of movement which
camera and cutting can handle with comparative ease. It
is the songs which set problems. The old convention of the
singer gliding from tree-trunk to tree-trunk, or from window
to window, entwining a pillar on the way, is out. Songs
are now choreographed. It is not uncommon these days to
have each line of a lyric sung against a different scenic
background. This is—and I am not being facetious—a
daring innovation, wholly cinematic and entirely valid if it
is related in style to the rest of the film. I do not mean the
whole film should be choreographed but it must have a sustained semblance of non-reality, and be played in a style
that makes for smooth transitions to the songs. Finally, I
should like to draw attention to the maestros who write the
lyrics and to those who set them to music (often a team of
two). I have been able to watch the development of the
Hindi film song over the years thanks to my son's continued interest in them. I keep on being amazed at the

inventiveness that is poured into them. As poetry they
are often no great shakes, but how many songs ever are?
In fact, one of the conditions of a good lyric is that it should
not be great poetry because a great poem carries its own
charge of music. But the really striking things are in the
tunes and in the orchestration. They first embrace all possible musical idioms—classical, folk, Negro, Greek, Punjabi,
Cha-Cha, or anything you can think of from any part of
the world. The latter shows a brashness and a verve in the
combination of instruments—again as disparate as you
can imagine—and a feeling for tonal colour and contrast
which call for high praise. And the main thing is that it
all makes sense as music, which is more than one can say of
a good deal of what is termed Modern Bengali Song.

It is perhaps the pressure of relentless output which
leads to an occasional 'appropriation'. But I feel less anger
than admiration for the composer who can lift the main
theme of the finest movement of Mozart's finest symphony,
turn it into a *filmi geet* and make it sound convincing.

1967

Meetings with a Maharaja 🖋

'Are you coming from Bombay?' asked the Maharaja.

'No,' I said, 'Calcutta.'

'This is a Bengali picture you're making?'

I sensed a tinge of disappointment in the Maharaja's demeanour. He took the vacant seat next to mine—one of the many sullen-looking sofas which lined the four walls of the Maharaja's sitting room. There were fluorescent tubes up near the four corners of the ceiling; half-a-dozen paintings of the calendar variety hung from various positions on the wall; a Kashmiri centre table had its brass top indecorously warped . . . it was hard to believe one was sitting in conference with the Maharaja of Jaisalmer, the oldest fortress town in western Rajasthan next to Chittor. Its bandit kings had once repulsed a siege by Alauddin Khilji. Would the present king resist an encroachment by a film company? I wondered.

'But why Jaisalmer?' asked the Maharaja. A moot question uttered in the flattest of drawls. Drink? Lethargy? Premature senility? (The Maharaja was barely forty.) The lustreless eyes beneath the drooping lids revealed nothing.

I said I had chosen Jaisalmer because (a) it was a most dramatic location perfectly answering the needs of our story, and (b) it had not been used by any other feature film makers before.

The Maharaja corrected us on the second point.

'They made a film here some years ago—*Sassi Punnu*. I think it was a Punjabi company.'

There was a silence. We waited for the Word. The Maharaja stirred. The drooping eyelids rose a millimetre or so.

'Well,' he said, getting up from the sofa, 'you may take photos.'

'Are there any dances in your film?' asked the Maharaja.

'Only a dance of demons. But not here. In Bengal, in a forest.'

The Maharaja smiled in slow motion. This was February. The last time we met was in December. In the meantime we had shot scenes in a Bengal village, in five feet deep snow up in Kufri in the Simla hills, in a desert flat as a sheet of plywood which stretched and stretched until it seemed to merge into an endless, waveless ocean which turned out to be a mirage that daily drew herds of thirsty deer to their death. Now we planned to shoot in the 800-year-old fortress town which would be Halla, the kingdom of the Bad King.

'I was told you needed some permission,' said the Maharaja.

'To shoot on the roof of the old palace,' I said, 'and to hoist some flags, with special emblems on them, at various points in the fort.'

'You won't displace mine?'

'No, no.'

'That's all right, then.'

'And we would like to use your big drum—the Bheri—for a war scene.'

'As long as you don't take it out of the fort.'

'And we want some camels.'

'How many?'

'Some hundreds—caparisoned—with men to ride them.'

The Maharaja seemed thoughtful for a minute. Then he turned to his cousin—the Kumar Bahadur.

'Get so-and-so to work on it. There should be no difficulty. Is that all?'

'That's all.'

'Oh yes. My daughter would like to watch your shooting. Please let him (pointing to the Kumar Bahadur) know your programme.'

'His Highness has arrived,' said someone, and I turned from the camels to see a jeep trundle up the hard, sandy slope and pull up right in front of the camel corps positioned for shooting. Luckily for the time being the camera faced the other way.

I walked up to the jeep and greeted the Maharaja.

'Good morning,' said His Highness. The smile lingered for a few seconds. 'So you're shooting.'

The Maharaja sat in the front seat. Right behind him was a curtain which shrouded the rear.

I excused myself and went back to the camels. The jeep held its position for a good half hour until a change of camera angle made it an intruder. A crowd thronged around the jeep. We cupped our hands over our mouths and shouted for the onlookers to move away. They shuffled off reluctantly. The jeep revved up and took a position outside the camera field. We kept shooting till 6-30: the days are long in Jaisalmer in March. By the time we finished the jeep had gone.

We sat, twelve of us, in the Maharaja's sitting room, sipping coffee and eating *ghulab jamons*.

'We make rasgullas too,' said the Maharaja.

We had finished our shooting and would be going away the next day.

'You must see the collection of manuscripts before you go. There are some of the oldest Jain manuscripts in the world in the vault below the temple.'

This was news. We had seen the temple but had no idea there was a vault underneath.

'And some of the havelis. There are wonderful old buildings in the city. They came and studied the plan of our city before they built Chandigarh.'

We were curious to know what the Maharaja's taste in films was like.

'I don't see many films. Only when I go to Delhi. But they are not so good these days. I liked *Parineeta* very much. And what was the other one? Also a Bengali story . . . yes —*Devdas*. Very artistic.'

The Maharaja now turned to Bagha Byne.

'Why didn't you bring your dholak? I saw you playing the dholak today. You should have brought it and played for us.'

A bearer came in with a tray with an assortment of stone objects on it: a tumbler, a teacup, a spoon, a necklace, some cuff-links. The gleaming purity of the saffron Jaisalmer marble made us hold our breath. It was as if gold had renounced its lustre and turned ascetic.

'Bring a bowl of water,' ordered the Maharaja, and the bearer obliged by bringing a blue plastic bowl half filled with water. The teacup and the tumbler were now gently placed in the water. They stayed on the surface, floating. It was like magic, and we all but applauded.

'They were made by a Muslim craftsman who is now dead. These were his last gifts to me. The only other craftsman who could carve them so thin and with such perfect balance has gone to Pakistan.'

The stone objects were taken out of the water and placed back on the table.

The Maharaja stirred. It was time for us to go.

'Today I could see that film making is very hard work. For some days now you must take complete rest.'

We had begun to file out of the room.

'You must come to Calcutta for the première of our film,' I said.

The Maharaja's eyes twinkled. He turned to Bagha again.

'Only if he promises to play the dholak.'

1968

An Indian New Wave? ✍

There is a belief gaining currency in film circles that a
New Wave of sorts is lapping on the shores of Indian
cinema. One reads about new directors, about low-cost and
non-star movies; one perks up at the sight of unfamiliar,
unadorned faces in the pages of film magazines; one even
hears of Art Theatres being planned to provide an outlet
for off-beat films. All of which is heartening indeed. It is
high time we had a Movement along the right lines, and
one wishes all power to those who are working to keep the
Wave from subsiding. The FFC, in particular, are showing
admirable courage and enterprise in providing loans to
young, untested applicants—as well as some old hands—
aspiring to make off-beat films.

While I have seen some of the results of this new enterprise, I do not wish to discuss them here in any specific
terms. The purpose of the present piece is to examine
some of the ideas which seem to be motivating the new
movement. These are being expressed by the film makers
themselves, as well as by some of the critics sympathetic to the trend. One can see them getting into a sort of
credo.

A key word in this credo is Experiment. Since experiment is at best a vague term meaning different things in
different contexts, it may be worthwhile to take a closer
look at it before going on to other things.

The early stages of the evolution of any language must necessarily be a process of trial and error; in other words, of experiment. Thus it would be right to say that the pioneers of the cinema were all experimenters. The cinema having been from the outset a visual medium of mass communication, experiment here took a special form. It was directed mainly towards tapping latent responses in the audience. It did not call for the evolution of new symbols, but for the pinpointing of familiar fragments of visible reality and endowing them with a particular meaning in a particular context. The audience was expected to 'read' a film in the way its maker intended it to be read. A film was thus a string of shots which worked like words and sentences and chapters in the unfolding of its story. And once it was realised that a cinema was a direct relation of the epic and the drama suitable for consumption by a large and varied public, the grammar of film making developed in a remarkably short time.

This rapid growth was possible because of a threefold pressure on the film maker. There was, first, his own urge for self-expression, common to all artists. Then there was the need to establish rapport with an audience, which brought it in line with the performing arts whose traditions stretched back two thousand years. This second pressure led to the evolution of a simple but forceful language, and to a choice of subjects with a broad appeal.

The third pressure was that of commerce. From the very beginning right down to the present, film makers have had to depend on sponsorship to provide them with the means of expression. It was really a case of mutual dependence: the film maker made his film from which the sponsor hoped to make a profit. Luckily this profit motive did not prove such a crippling handicap for the artist, because it was soon realised that, as in all other performing arts, it was possible in the cinema too to strike a satisfactory balance between art and commerce.

The question of esotericism simply did not arise in the early days. The cinema was accepted by all concerned as a popular art which drew its sustenance from the paying public. It was as simple as that. In the circumstances, naturally, all experiment was directed towards enriching the language in order to heighten its impact. The fact that we laugh at the films of Chaplin and Keaton is not just because they were funny men doing funny things in funny situations, but because they were great artists and great experimenters who discovered the cinematic methods to turn a funny scene on paper into a funny scene on the screen.

There is no such thing as an effect for its own sake in the films of the old masters. The true artist is recognisable in his style and his attitude, not in his idiosyncrasies. Occasionally, a great artist failed to make contact with his audience. Such was Erich von Stroheim, and we now know the reason for it. Stroheim was trying to purvey a ruthless cynicism to a public which was simply not ready for it. Today Stroheim emerges as a giant, a true experimenter.

Experiment in the period of sound was directed precisely towards the same end as in the silent era—namely, how to make the medium more eloquent. The pressures were the same as before and the progress just as rapid.

Sound, as we know, brought the cinema closer to nature. It also did something else. By introducing the spoken word, it took away some of its universality and introduced an element of regionalism. The concept of a national cinema with a national style emerged more forcefully now than in the silent period. No wonder that the nation most noted for its sophistication should at this time have seen the most sophisticated developments in its cinema. For experiment on an adult level in the early period of sound, one has to turn to France and, more particularly, to Jean Renoir.

It is significant that Renoir has named only one director as his mentor: Erich von Stroheim. It was not Stroheim's cynicism that Renoir imbibed, but his sharp observation of human behaviour, his use of details, and his fearless probing of truth. These are qualities which one associated with the serious novel rather than with the erstwhile cinema. The film that best epitomises Renoir is *La Règle du Jeu*, made in 1939. More than any other film, *La Règle du Jeu* contained the seeds of the *avant-garde* that was to emerge twenty years later. Under a genial and relaxed exterior, the film was a mordant satire on the French aristocracy of the time. There was a lot of talk in it, but it could never have been a play; there was much searching analysis, but it could not have made a novel; even the screenplay reveals only a fraction of its treasures. *La Règlé du Jeu* is wholly cinematic. Its plot is of a kind that defies summarisation in seven words (Hollywood's one-time criterion of a good screen story). Although perfectly comprehensible on the surface, *La Règle du Jeu* is a difficult and demanding film. In its various layers of meaning, it achieved a density which was unknown in the cinema of its time. One has constantly to read between the lines and, like all great works of art, one has to go back to it again and again to discover fresh nuances of meaning. Even if there had been no technical and syntactical innovations in the film, *La Règle* would still have been an *advanced* film by virtue of its content alone. But there are other innovations as well, and they are so well integrated into the texture of the film that one hardly notices them. For instance, deep focus—a common enough device nowadays —was used by Renoir for the first time in *La Règle du Jeu*. This came about when Renoir found that the nature of the story occasionally called for different actions unfolding simultaneously in the same shot in different depths of field. The only way in which equal emphasis could be bestowed on these actions was by extending the focus to cover a greater depth than was customary in indoor photography of that time.

Within a few years of Renoir, and independently of him, another innovator—this time in the United States—was to use deep focus extensively in his very first film. In *Citizen Kane*, Orson Welles wanted an overall sharpness in all his images, and his gifted cameraman Gregg Toland had to devise new lenses in order to achieve it. Welles wished, in a sense, to 'spare no details' in this ruthless study of an American tycoon.

Both *Kane* and *La Règle* treaded on too many corns for their own safety, and both were denied immediate success at the box office. Today no one questions their right to be regarded as milestones in the history of the cinema.

The first emergence of a school with a name happened in Italy in the immediate post-war years. The Neo-Realists were led by writers who were professed Leftists (Zavattini, Sergio Amidei). Their experiment consisted in bringing the film story down to the level of everyday reality. To match the treatment with the concept, directors like De Sica, Rossellini, Lattuada and Castellani took their cameras out in the streets and engaged non-actors (mostly) to play leading roles. We know that the films won both success and acclaim, but perhaps not enough thought has been given to the reasons for it. The main reasons were three—(a) the scripts turned out by the writers had superbly organised classical structures; (b) they were deeply human in content; and (c) the directors, particularly Rossellini and De Sica, were first-rate craftsmen with years of solid achievement behind them. If *Bicycle Thieves* looks shoddy, it is only on the surface: the post-war film stock and processing in Italy were both less than satisfactory. Anyone who studies a film by De Sica will marvel at the ease and fluency of his mise-en-scène.

The fifties found Hollywood shaking in its shoes while TV slowly lured the audience away from the movie theatres. The only experiment that took place at this time had to do with the inflation of the screen ratio. The adult and serious work in the cinema was confined to a handful of directors in Europe and—as *Rashomon* proved—in Japan.

This was the time of the emergence of the New Wave in France. On the crest of the wave rode some young critics from the staff of the most distinguished film journal in Europe—*Cahiers du Cinéma*. The reason why the New Wave happened in France and not elsewhere is the same as why *La Règle du Jeu* happened in France: it is the only country in the world where a departure from the norm in art is not immediately scoffed at.

Not that all the New Wave directors were unconventional to the same extent. Some of the early films of Claude Chabrol, for instance, have the surface of slick Hollywood products. Truffaut's beautiful *400 Blows* has passages of great originality; but the structure beneath the apparently episodic story is fairly conventional. The one thorough-going iconoclast in the group was Jean-Luc Godard. As an innovator, one has to put him not far below D. W. Griffith, and any analysis of the New Wave unorthodoxy must in the end boil down to an analysis of the methods of Jean-Luc Godard.

Godard decided that films could be made cheaply and quickly, and then set out boldly to work out what conventional items of expense could be dispensed with without destroying the essential purity of the art form. In effect, this was a fresh exploration of the fundamentals of film making, and it involved the questioning of all known methods and trying out new ones in their places. As *Breathless* and subsequent films proved, Godard was perfectly justified in applying rough and ready methods to films which dealt basically with unconventional people in an unconventional era. In other words, the Godard form grew out of the Godard content, and the Godard content has always embraced some aspect of contemporary European youth—journalist, soldier, prostitute, working girl, intellectual—caught in the whirl of modern living. The syntax is new, the pace and rhythm are new, the conception of narrative is new.

Godard is the first director in the history of the cinema to have totally dispensed with what is known as the plot line. Indeed, it would be right to say that Godard has devised a totally new genre for the cinema. This genre cannot be defined, it can only be described. It is a *collage* of story, tract, newsreel, reportage, quotations, allusions, commercial short, and straight TV interview—all related to a character or a set of characters firmly placed in a precise contemporary milieu. A cinema of the head and not of the heart, and therefore, a cinema of the minority.

The means by which Godard is able to discard plot is simply by doing away with the kind of obligatory scenes which would set the audience speculating on possible lines of development. This forces one not to anticipate but only to watch and absorb.

Let me give an example. *Masculine-Feminine* opens in a restaurant where a boy and a girl, sitting at separate tables set at least twenty feet apart, strike up an acquaintance. They talk, but since the camera is at a distance from them, and since there is heavy traffic on the street outside (seen through the glass door), we do not make out what they are

saying. Godard here reverses convention by keeping the
noise of the traffic deliberately and, if I may say so, realistically, above the level of conversation. This goes on for
some time when suddenly a man gets up from another table,
walks out of the restaurant, and is immediately followed
by a woman who takes out a pistol from her handbag and
shoots him down at point-blank range. The boy and the
girl make some inaudible comments on this, and the scene
ends. It remains to add that the boy and the girl continue
to be the focal point of the film, while the murder is never
brought up again.

At a cursory viewing, it would be easy to dismiss the
scene as pointless and incoherent. But on second thoughts
(or perhaps second viewing), it might begin to dawn on
one that the scene not only presents actuality in a more
truthful way than one is used to in the cinema, but it also
makes some valid comments on our life and times. Film
grammar tells us that essentials should be stressed, and
enumerates the various audio-visual ways of doing so; but
what if a director has a totally new angle on what is essential and what is not? In the scene just described, what has
been established beyond dispute is that a boy and a girl
met in a restaurant and talked. What they said is, to
Godard, inessential. It is also established that while they sat
talking a woman murdered a man (Husband? Lover?—
inessential) within their sight. Now, it is customary for directors to arrange background action for their scenes where
such action is called for. This usually takes the form of unobtrusive but characteristic bits of business which make up
a credible atmosphere without disturbing the main lines
of action in the foreground. But what if someone uses an
extremely violent bit of action in the *background*, if only
to suggest that we live in an age where violence is all around
us? And the youthful pair's apparent unconcern—does

it not suggest the apathy to violence which can grow out of a prolonged exposure to a climate of extreme violence?

It is important to note that with Godard the reversal of convention is not a gimmick or an affectation, but a positive and meaningful extension of the film language.

Godard is fully aware that he treads on dangerous ground when he drops all pretence of telling a story. But being as much concerned about the audience as anybody else, he provides attractive handholds for them to latch on to in the absence of a story line. Among these are the telling details which breathe life into the shots, superb action from all the performers (stars even—for what else is Jean Paul Belmondo?), and quick changes of mood achieved with wit, grace and style.

In his recent films, Godard has sacrificed art for politics; but even in his best and most characteristic early works, he has been a bad model for young directors simply because his kind of cinema demands craftsmanship of the highest order, let alone various other equipments on an intellectual plane. In order to turn convention upside down, one needs a particularly firm grip on convention itself. This Godard had, thanks to years of assiduous film studying at the Cinémathèque in Paris. Those who have seen his first short story film *Every Man is Called Patrick* know what a sure grasp of narrative he had before he made *Breathless*.

The late sixties have seen the collapse of the System in Hollywood and the rise of young unconventional directors in place of the old guard. An *Easy Rider* shows how far Hollywood can move away from convention and yet pack them in. The new US youth audience is of course a special breed. We cannot yet measure exactly what drugs have done to alter the response of this audience. Part of the

success of a film like *Easy Rider* must be due to a qualitative
change in this response. At the same time, one should not
discount the presence in the film of elements which would
be affecting even for a conventional audience with its
conventional demands. *Easy Rider* may not have a story,
but it does, after its own fashion, make a statement, and
a moving one at that. It also has its quota of sex, some
violence, a pop song in the background, and three superb
performances by potential stars.

It is significant that in the cinema of the West the veering towards unconventionalism has been exactly simul-
taneous with the growth of permissiveness. All young
directors, whether in Europe or USA or Japan (even Eastern
Europe, as some Czech films have shown), have exploited
this permissiveness in their so-called off-beat films. It is
also significant that 'fragmentation'—a modish cinematic
device which chops up a scene or a statement—has rarely
been applied to scenes of sexual encounter. In other words,
the new experimentalists and iconoclasts abroad have
come up—thanks to changed social attitudes—with their
own formulae for survival in a commercial set-up. So the
breaking of convention goes merrily along, while the box
office is taken care of by permissive sex.

Which brings us to our own country where, alas, such
permissiveness is still a long way off. And yet the New
Wave is being talked about and the off-beat film is on the
way to becoming a reality.

The first question to ask at this point would be: how
does one define off-beat in the context of Indian cinema;
or, more specifically, of Hindi cinema, since much of the
activity seems to be centred in Bombay?

The ingredients of the average Hindi film are well known;
colour (Eastman preferred); songs (six or seven?) in voices
one knows and trusts; dance—solo and ensemble—the

more frenzied the better; bad girl, good girl, bad guy, good guy, romance (but no kisses); tears, guffaws, fights, chases, melodrama; characters who exist in a social vacuum; dwellings which do not exist outside the studio floor; locations in Kulu, Manali, Ooty, Kashmir, London, Paris, Hong Kong, Tokyo... who needs to be told? See any three Hindi films, and two will have all the ingredients listed above. This may well be the classical nine *rasas* prescription carried to its nth limit of crudity. But the fervour and frequency with which this prescription is applied suggests that it has become like a game with a set of rules which is being played by both the backers and the makers of the films, and played in a spirit of intense and engrossing rivalry. Although one may play for very high stakes and lose, one never thinks of questioning the rules of the game, as one never questions those of bridge or chess or cricket.

In the circumstances, assuming that you are given a chance to make an off-beat film in Hindi, you will have made one by just leaving out any four of the ingredients listed above. And such films *are* made from time to time (*Anand*, and the first part of *Mera Naam Joker* are recent examples). But surely this is a far cry from the off-beat in the European sense? This provokes my second question: is an *avant-garde* in the European sense a viable proposition in India? In France, the Malraux ministry at one time subsidised some eminent but 'difficult' directors. Bresson was one of them. Is there any likelihood of such subsidy here, assuming that we too have 'difficult' directors of the widely acknowledged calibre of Bresson? I doubt it.

If one studies the young *avant-garde* abroad that functions within the 35 mm commercial set-up (as opposed to Underground, where the normal laws of supply and demand do not operate), one notices the element of permissive sex applied as a safeguard in nine cases out of ten. The established serious directors are spared this constraint simply because their names carry their own guarantee of reliability, which usually also implies the guarantee of a well-thought-out, well-made, well-cast, well-advertised product.

We in India would be wise not to ignore the implications of this overall pattern. I am thinking particularly of the young iconoclasts who hope to find that 2 or $2\frac{1}{2}$ lakhs of rupees for the non-conformist masterpiece they have been dreaming of. I should have thought that such a sum of money would be a heavy burden for an artist to carry for any length of time. I am glad that the Film Finance Corporation have taken the stand that they have; and it is because they have done so that it now devolves on the film makers to bear in mind certain limitations they have to face, the 'conventions' that even they have to follow. Having worked for twenty years on as many films, and seen both success and failure over a wide range of subjects, I think I have earned the right to set out what these conventions and limitations are.

Two assumptions are necessary before we can proceed: one—the off-beaters will have no access to permissive sex for a long time yet; and two—art theatres will come into existence to provide an outlet for their films when the need arises. In other words, we shall continue to toe the puritanical-hypocritical line, and not depend wholly on normal channels of distribution and exhibition.

I think one has also to assume that when our young film makers talk of non-conformism, they are not thinking of minor deviations from the norm, but of radical ones. Whatever the extent of deviation, they have to remember that off-beat, like most other things in life, comes in three varieties— good, bad and indifferent. The second has no chance of

success anywhere at any time. Trash of the *conventional*
type may succeed, but never the off-beat. I understand
the new film makers are pinning their faith on the perceptive minority, and the hunt is to track them down and
turn them into patrons of the proposed art theatres. Do
these film makers seriously believe that this minority is
tucked away in odd corners of the country and have only to
be ferreted out of their holes to make a beeline for these
art theatres? My own belief is they are all around us, within
easy reach and in enough numbers to make a two-lakh proposition pay, waiting for the right kind of off-beat movie
to turn up.

What is this right kind of off-beat? Here, I am afraid,
the film makers do not help us very much. They talk of
experiment without clearly specifying what lines the experiment is to take and how far it is to go. One only hears
of low budget, of short shooting schedules, and of the avoidance of stars. One also hears occasionally of improvisation
and of doing away with the story.

Experience would suggest that some of these are mutually
annihilating concepts. But let us first examine them, starting
with the most dangerous and deluding concept: Improvisation.

To me the word can mean one of two things: one, the
film maker has thought it all out; but because he has not
set it down on paper for others to read, he can *pretend* to
be improvising. This is a form of artistic dishonesty which
may or may not work against the film. But when one works
with small funds, *writing it down beforehand cuts costs*. The
second meaning: the film maker does not want to think
ahead because he is confident of being inventive at the
last moment. This provokes the following set of questions:
(*a*) If the film maker is not thinking of the film he is about
to make, what is he thinking of? (*b*) If he does not think

ahead, how is he going to plan and work out how much it is going to cost?, and (c) If he does his thinking at the last moment, where is the time for the others to think—the actors, the cameraman, the assistants? Or is the thinking of all these people of such small concern that it can be dispensed with?

Every director who is not a hack improvises to a certain extent within a defined scheme. Actors' gestures, camera movements, camera set-ups, bits of dialogue, background action—not all of these can be set down in advance precisely on paper. Striking ideas may turn up at the last moment and be used. But the person who talks of improvisation as a guiding principle in film making is more likely than not to be incapable of thinking at any time.

Let us now take the convention of the story. Considering its lusty existence for well over two thousand years, it seems naive to believe that the last ten years or so have somehow seen the demise of the story. Only when human beings undergo mutation to a new species will their normal collective demands be replaced by something else. The love of narrative, in no matter what disguised form, is too deeply ingrained in the human species. It is true that the audience has changed in the last fifty years, and equally true that film makers have discovered a hundred different ways of telling a story where there were only a dozen. This is a phenomenal growth compared with, say, that of literature. The development of language from Griffith to Godard in films is roughly equivalent to that from Chaucer to Joyce in English literature—a matter of 600 years as against 60 in the cinema. Godard ushered in the contemporary idiom. This idiom has been partly absorbed into the film language of today. But in spite of the changed idiom, the convention of narrative in whatever shape or form has remained. Every film is *about* something

—usually about people, who pass through various phases and events which give the film a shape. This, to me, is a story. Anyone who thinks that a story is a lot of plot that twists and turns and rises and falls has got the wrong definition for today. By discarding the story altogether one would be destroying the very basis of a film that a lot of people are expected to see and like.

I would even suggest that a film maker who wishes to use the modern idiom has even greater need of a simple framework. As I understand it, the modern idiom is marked by a greater density than the old one. More is said in less space and less time. A terse, muscular, elliptic idiom. But the trouble is that for an audience to catch up with it, there is a difficulty that is inherent in the film medium itself. Let me explain by drawing a comparison with literature. Here is a random extract from *Ulysses*:

> Flood of warm jimjam lickitup secretness flowed to flow in music out, in desire, dark to lick flow, invading. Tipping her tepping her tapping her topping her. Tup. Pores to dilate dilating. Tup. The joy the feel the warm the. Tup. To pour over sluices pouring gushes. Flood, gush, flow, joygush, tupthrop. Now! Language of love.

This cannot be read like light fiction if one is to make any sense of it. A reader who refuses to grapple with this kind of language is free to shut the book and put it away. One who does not must be prepared to take his time. *But a film-goer's time is not his own time.* Everything in the cinema, every kind of film—comic, tragic, light, serious, conventional, experimental—unreels at the constant speed of twenty-four frames per second. One cannot shut the film and think. One cannot go back to the passage, savour that imagery or turn of phrase, ponder over that allusion and trace it to its source.

If this is understood, my plea for a simple subject to go with a modern idiom will also be understood. After all, even Joyce needed the framework of a classical myth. Even the most elite minority audience will look for something to get their teeth into. Assuming that our *avant-garde* do not wish to alienate this audience, they will have to provide a balm along with the irritant. Such a balm is a simple subject, and such another is a star.

Perhaps the shrillest voices of the new film makers have been raised against the stars. I do not know what definition of a star these film makers have been using, but mine goes something like this: a star is a person on the screen who continues to be expressive and interesting even after he or she has stopped doing anything. This definition does not exclude the rare and lucky breed that gets five or ten lakhs of rupees per film; and it includes anyone who keeps his calm before the camera, projects a personality and evokes empathy. This is a rare breed too, but one has met it in our films. Suhasini Mulay of *Bhuvan Shome* is such a star; so is Dhritiman Chatterji of *Pratidwandi*; so are the two girls of *Uski Roti*.

The advantage of having such a star, especially for the off-beat film maker, is truly immense. One has only to remember the magnetism lent to unconventional films by actors like Belmondo, Jean-Pierre Leaud, Anna Karina, Jeanne Moreau, Czybulski, Jack Nicholson. There is only one director in the world who has made an absolute fetish of using non-actors, and anyone who has seen a Bresson film and observed the Bresson faces knows with what care he chooses his 'types'. Care in the casting of actors—professional or non-professional—is a *sine qua non* of the healthy existence of an *avant-garde*.

And care in craftsmanship too. By craftsmanship I do not mean the superficial gloss, which one can well do without. I mean the most effective use of the means at one's disposal. I am thinking particularly of the avoidance of the kind of shoddiness which is the equivalent of clumsy prose in writing which can mean either lack of education or lack of clear thinking or both. If the shooting is haphazard, if the images are shoddy, how can it all add up to an effective and meaningful statement? By inspired editing? Is it possible to arrange a series of clumsy sentences into meaningful literature?

One can cut out the conventional story with its conventional line and substitute a patchwork of ideas *à la* Godard. But even a patchwork has its own aesthetic laws, violating which will only result in a grotesque. And we know what *that* means in art. 'Take the head of a horse, the torso of an elephant, the hind legs of a camel . . .' began Da Vinci's recipe for drawing a monster. It is doubtful if the discriminating minority will go for a hybrid if they can find the meat in a conventional movie.

The temptation to try and get away with it is strong in the unconventional film maker. Since there is no norm for the off-beat, his work cannot be measured against one. Therefore, he can always *claim* that he has done something new and meaningful. But unless his claim is endorsed by the perceptive minority, the work of art will remain un-vindicated. Individual responses are of small ultimate value to a film maker. If his own claim is justified, sooner or later endorsement will come from perhaps an even wider circle than he bargained for.

Unfortunately, the kind of movement that we need here must set its targets in the present and not in posterity. That is why the film maker must be prepared to deal with the collective mind, with collective response. This collective response is a peculiar thing which may have nothing to do with what a certain critic or a certain member of the film maker's coterie thinks of his work. Let us say that X is the individual response that extols this work, and Y the one that runs it down. X will provide the film maker with the boost that all artists need, and Y the exasperation that is also his heritage. Both X and Y may be contained in the collective response, but the sum total of response is likely to be neither X nor Y, but Z—a third new entity. All film makers aim at arousing in the audience that mysterious thing of the mind called empathy, which is the opposite of being left cold; Z is in direct ratio to this empathy. And it is Z which ultimately decides the fate of a film even under ideal conditions of making and showing it.

In the circumstances, the only sensible thing for the artist to do is to be objective to the extent that he may rise above his personal idiosyncrasies. The audience will put up with the showiest of directors provided his matter justifies his manner. The modern idiom, unless backed by a genuinely modern attitude to life and society, is apt to degenerate into gimmickry and empty flamboyance. Renoir revealed this attitude in *La Règle du Jeu*, so did Welles in *Citizen Kane*, so does Godard in film after film. It is necessary to point out that the New Wave was marked as much by a new syntax as by a new philosophy.

All in all, I am less worried about the film makers aiming too high—which is not a bad thing—than aiming the wrong way. I am not sure I am happy about the minority audience syndrome either. This seems suspiciously like a defensive manoeuvre on the part of the new film makers. Why not aim wider? I do not know of a single film maker who has been dismayed by a wide acceptance of his work.

However, if the film makers insist on this elusive minority, they must remember that this minority, in India, is likely to be somewhat less educated filmwise, and for obvious reasons, than its European counterpart. This audience will expect, firstly, a modicum of craftsmanship, which can be achieved within a low budget and a short time only with the help of know-how and meticulous planning; secondly, they will expect a star or stars (vide my definition); and thirdly, a subject with the basic attributes of contrast and interplay of credible human emotions capable of arousing empathy. The film should also cover the conventional minimum of a ninety-minute span without undue and obvious padding. One can think of shorter features only under conditions of lowered seat prices to go with them. This is logical. In the book trade, for instance, other things being equal, a slim book costs less than a fat one regardless of author and quality.

Among recent films, *Bhuvan Shome* is cited widely as an off-beat film which has succeeded with a minority audience. My own opinion is that whatever success it has had has not been because of, but in spite of its new aspects. It worked because it used some of the most popular conventions of cinema which helped soften the edges of its occasional spiky syntax. These conventions are: a delectable heroine, an ear-filling background score, and a simple, wholesome, wish-fulfilling screen story (summary in seven words: Big Bad Bureaucrat Reformed by Rustic Belle).

However, there may be a pointer here for the new film makers. *Bhuvan Shome* may well define the kind of off-beat most likely to succeed with our minority audience—the kind that *looks* a bit like its French counterpart, but is essentially old-fashioned and Indian beneath its trendy habit.

1971

Four and a Quarter 🖋

Four Hindi features and a wordless short, seen in the space of the last few months. The short bears the seal of Films Division, but is still very much a personal statement. The features were made outside the pale of the commercial industry. Three—*Garam Hawa*, *Mayadarpan* and *Duvidha* —were made under the FFC, while *Ankur* was privately financed.

The four films pair off conveniently. *Garam Hawa* and *Ankur* are both in the tradition of narrative cinema, although both depart widely from the normal pattern of Hindi films. *Duvidha* and *Mayadarpan* preserve the narrative framework, but are otherwise emphatically non-traditional. *Garam Hawa* being the only film to have been seen by the public at the time of writing, I shall deal with it first.

In the context of a largely themeless Hindi cinema, *Garam Hawa* goes to the other extreme of taking a story (by Ismat Chughtai) which for its theme alone would have made the film a milestone, even if it lacked other qualities. It concerns a Moslem family in Agra just after the Partition. The social and political pressures brought to bear upon it form the substance of the story. The central character is the gentle, dignified Salim Mirza, owner of a shoe factory, who keeps shrugging off the occasional signs of hostility as something which will 'pass off in a few days'.

The other members of the family are his wife, a pillar of strength and a model of fortitude; his aged mother, who strains her near-deaf ears to catch snippets of the latest gossip filtering through the screen; his daughter, who finds time for romance amidst her household chores; and his young college-student son who imbibes leftist notions which pave the way for the note of hope at the end of the tragic tale.

Mirza's optimism proves to be short-lived. The social boycott begins to take concrete forms and pressure piles upon pressure. The bank refuses overdraft; orders for shoes are cancelled; near-riot ensues as a result of the family *tonga* accidentally upsetting a fruit vendor's cart in a Hindu *mohalla*. Mirza begins to buckle under the strain. The ancestral *haveli* has to be abandoned, and the family moves into a smaller house in a new locality. Mother, her hearth and home gone, feels life ebbing out of her. A *palki* ride through tortuous lanes brings her temporarily back to her beloved home where, in answer to her wish, she breathes her last.

With his daughter taking her own life, Mirza's hopes vanish. Father, mother and son pack their belongings and set off for the railway station. They will cross the border, as others have done. The *tonga* pulls up as a procession appears with a red flag and crosses its path. Son makes a quick decision. He will join the procession, stay back and fight for communal harmony. Mirza too steps out, ponders for a while, and decides to follow suit.

The pattern of events in *Garam Hawa* is not unique—a notable precedent being *Professor Mamlock*—but it serves the purpose of the story extremely well. Director Sathyu's handling of it—except in a couple of extended and expendable passages in the second half—is calm, assured and entirely free from frills. There is no sign of effort in

the way sympathy is built up, and no didacticism. And in
all this he is helped enormously by his cast, which stays on
the right pitch throughout. If Balraj Sahni as Salim Mirza
stands out with his quiet authority and magnificent presence, the other members of his family are no less memorable for the sincerity and conviction with which they
perform in what happens to be their first screen appearances.
The Agra locations are beautifully handled, which suggests
that Sathyu not only has a feel for them but knows how
to use them to the best advantage of the story. There are
evidences that the film was made with small resources; but
the occasional rough edge which results from it is more
than compensated by the air of single-minded devotion
which permeates the whole film.

Ankur, too, like *Garam Hawa*, happens to be the first
feature film of its director, Shyam Benegal. It is about a
young boy from the city who comes to live in his father's
farm, and is drawn slowly but inexorably towards the
maid-servant wife of a deaf-mute farmhand. The husband
is drummed out of the village in punishment for an offence.
In his absence the girl sleeps with the hero and conceives.
To add to the hero's dilemma, his newly married wife
arrives at this point and immediately resents the proximity
of the young and attractive servant girl. The farmhand,
too, returns from his exile and adds unwittingly to the
complications. Fearing exposure, the cornered hero decides on a volte-face as a face-saving strategy, and takes
cowardly refuge in a gratuitous physical assault on the
helpless deaf-mute.

As even the bare outline suggests, *Ankur* is not free from
melodrama. Benegal makes the mistake of turning the
scales too heavily against the hero towards the end, with
nothing in the early part to suggest that he is capable
of such monstrosity. As a result he ends up as a rather

trite symbol of urban pollution invading the pure air of the country. The whole denouement has the air of being conceived as a forced rounding-off of a story whose normal course would have led to an impasse. As a firm believer in geometry as a guiding principle in art, I should strongly advise Benegal to keep away from quadrangles in the future.

Story apart, *Ankur* has enough qualities to make one look forward to Benegal's future with keen anticipation. For one thing, he shows great confidence in the handling of two major elements of film making: acting and camera. In the latter case, the static shots are as well judged as the mobile ones, and ensures that interest is sustained even through comparatively uneventful passages. There is a long section early on, beginning with the hero's arrival on the farm, where nothing very much happens from a narrative point of view, but it is held together by a profusion of details, by touches of comedy, and by the carefully handled relationship between the hero and the farmhand's wife— spatially distant yet charged with the possibility of closer contact, with all its implications in terms of plot and drama.

Shabana Azmi, who plays the farmhand's wife, does not immediately fit into her rustic surroundings; but her poise and her personality are never in doubt, and in two high-pitched scenes she pulls out all the stops and firmly establishes herself as one of our finest dramatic actresses.

Dramatic acting is something which will not be found in Mani Kaul's *Duvidha*; nor, for that matter, in Kumar Shahani's *Mayadarpan*. One questions if what one finds instead can be called acting at all. In Kaul's case the answer is an unequivocal no, and I think Kaul himself will agree with me only too readily. We shall deal with Shahani later.

Kaul has made two features before *Duvidha*, of which one, *Uski Roti*, I have seen. On the evidence of these two films there is no doubt that Kaul has wilfully adopted a very special and very private mode of expression. As the first director in the history of Indian cinema to have done so, he is a phenomenon to be reckoned with. He has not only done away with most of the clichés of narrative cinema, but with most of its axioms too. Surprisingly enough, he has not discarded narrative itself. What concerns us is the sum total of what remains. Here is an outline of the haunting little Rajasthani folk-tale which serves as the basis of *Duvidha*:

A young lad goes to look for work in a distant town, leaving his newly married wife behind. In his absence the wife encounters a ghost who turns out to be a flesh and blood replica of her husband. They live together, and in time a child is born. Husband's return precipitates a first class dilemma on a personal as well as a social plane. The vexed question of who is the real husband is at last solved by exorcism. The ghost-husband is trapped in a bag and flung into a deep well. Real husband returns to wife and child.

In its mysterious, almost surrealist quality, the tale is on a par with some of the best of the Vetala stories. One can imagine a professional teller of folk-tales revelling in the bizarre goings on and artfully manipulating the listeners' sympathies between husband, wife and ghost, with all his efforts directed towards one single aim—that of gripping his audience. He would doubtless succeed, because a story such as this, lying beyond the pale of rationality and deriving its special haunting quality from it, is best told in words, whether written or spoken, where the recipient's imagination can have a free play. If it is to work in a visual medium, then the idiom has to be either highly articulate, with full emphasis on the human element, and with all the resources of magic and mood and atmosphere at full play; or far more stylised and *outré* than the one Kaul adopts for the film. Kaul's impatience with conventional narrative methods leads him to a visual style replete with clichés of another sort. Shot in Rajasthan and in colour, the film revels in compositions which, before they have conveyed their meaning, have sounded their echoes of all that is chic in modern advertising photography. *Duvidha* abounds in red silk and yellow turbans and white wall surfaces and tremulous eardrops and mehndi-painted hands and black eyelashes on black eyes demurely downcast or raised in a querulous glance. This is self-indulgence, and as such incompatible with any sort of discipline.

That is why Kaul's reduction of the human element to faces and minimal gestures, to crowds seen from the back or from above (hence the clusters of turbans), seems to be the result of a plain lack of interest in human beings. The gesture which Kaul most frequently allows his actors is a slow turn of the head from one profile to the other, which is itself reduced to a cliché in no time. An unerring choice of types might have provided some compensation, but here too Kaul fails in a key role—that of the bride. The one normal human act she performs—that of eating —betrays her urbanity instantly.

The full-bodied folk-songs on the sound track suggest that it is only human beings on screen which Kaul cringes from. The rest of the sound track consists of—(*a*) long passages of total silence, (*b*) a commentary which helps the story along, (*c*) selective synchronous sounds, and (*d*) dialogue which is largely overlapped. The sparseness of the sound track invests some of the rare synchronous effects with a significance (the jingle of coins as a hand

8

receives money) which turns them into little pockets of pleasure. Photographically, the one valid, original device consists in the careful use of available light which turns the ghost-husband into a dark presence with glinting eyes. In the final passages of the film leading to the exorcism, Kaul attempts a heightening of pitch by using the sound of shuffling feet over shots of villagers hurrying to the well. This is, of course, tantamount to a hearty meal compared to the starvation diet of the rest of the film; but the symptoms of pernicious anaemia linger. One does not have to be an all-in wrestler to prove that one is healthy; the lean ascetic can be healthy too, but only through the discipline of yoga. Kaul's wayward, fragile aestheticism has led him to the sick-bed.

And likewise Kumar Shahani. It is strange that both Kaul and Shahani should acknowledge their debt to Ritwik Ghatak, who taught them at Poona, when the only Ghatak trait they seem to have imbibed is a lack of humour. In every other respect—in their avoidance of strong situations and full-blooded characters, in their lack of concern for social issues, in their use of camera and cutting, there is not a trace of Ghatak to be discerned. Shahani's other allegiance is to Bresson with whom he had worked on a film. The legacy of that lesson is to be seen in the girl in the centre of *Mayadarpan*. She, too, like Mouchette, suffers inwardly and wordlessly. No quarrel with that. But we are concerned with what happens outwardly. And here, I am afraid, Bresson evaporates.

Does Shahani seriously believe that the major outward manifestation of such suffering is a slow, rigid ambulation up and down verandas repeated every five minutes or so throughout the film? Film language would be threatened with extinction if this were really so. To me *Mayadarpan* seems a combination of poor psychology and poorer stylisation. Even the sophisticated response to colour goes for nothing in a film that is so gauche in its handling of the human element. Even more than Kaul, Shahani seems to forget that when one imposes a rigid style on the actor without a thorough working out of its expressive possibilities, it becomes indistinguishable from bad acting. The method becomes extremely risky in a story with an urban background, where the nature of life and work severely limits the range of expressive gestures. The only possible approach here is the psychological one, for which Shahani seems to have no use.

In the same programme with *Mayadarpan* was *Koodal*, a short by the Delhi painter Tyeb Mehta. *Koodal* shows a much better grasp of the film medium than that other film by a painter : Husain's *Through the Eyes of a Painter*. Not that I was on the same wave-length with the film all the way through: the relevance of the sustained shot of the maker himself crossing a busy street seemed particularly elusive in a film dealing largely with cows; nevertheless, the film pleases as much by its response to forms, textures and moods (the scene in the empty slaughterhouse is very well done indeed), as by the way it is cut for cohesion to Narayana Menon's Carnatic score.

1974

THEIR FILMS

Renoir in Calcutta ✍

My decision to see Renoir at his hotel was a more or less desperate one. Although his arrival in Calcutta had been marked by a conspicuous lack of publicity, the stir it had created among local students of the cinema was considerable. For this was no chance visit. Renoir's mission was here, in Calcutta. He had come with the professed intention of making a film of Rumer Godden's novel, *The River*, against authentic backgrounds in Bengal.

But fame invests a man with an aura of unapproachability, and I had all but despaired of a chance of meeting the great director when I stumbled upon Clyde de Vinna. A wizened, wisecracking American, De Vinna had acquired some reputation and a great deal of experience in the early nineteen-thirties by photographing *Trader Horn*. He was now considered something of an expert in outdoor photography, and had been engaged to supervise the preliminary shooting of *The River* (in monopack Technicolor). De Vinna had allayed my misgivings by cheerfully asserting that 'John is a great guy, a great individualist, and very approachable. You can see him any day at his hotel in the evening.'

As it turned out, Renoir was not only approachable, but so embarrassingly polite and modest that I felt if I were not too careful I would probably find myself discoursing upon the Future of the Cinema for his benefit. There were

so many things I wanted to ask him. Why did he want to
make *The River*? Did he enjoy making films in Hollywood?
But when it came to asking them I found that I was hope-
lessly mixed up, and came out with something inane like:
How did he like India?

Renoir replied with great seriousness: 'That I will tell
you when I have known it better. At present I am only
beginning to understand the city of Calcutta, which I find
very interesting.' Renoir had a great deal to say about the
two or three trips he had already made around the city and
on the Ganges. The river, with its old-fashioned boats, had
charmed him, and he was fascinated by all the colourful
things he had seen. 'You know,' he said, 'India seems to
have retained some of the charm and simplicity of primitive life. The way the boatmen pull the oars, and the
farmers plough the fields, and the women draw water from
the wells, they remind you of old Egyptian murals and
bas-relief.'

Renoir had met a family of refugees who had come all
the way from Pakistan by boat. 'And they had all sorts of
fantastic adventures on the way,' he said. 'I am sure their
story would make a very good film.' I said India was full
of such stories which simply cried out for filming. 'And
no doubt they are going to be made,' said Renoir with
naive conviction. I said, 'No, because the Indian director
seems to find more inspiration in the slick artificiality of a
Hollywood film than in the reality around him.' 'Ah, the
American film . . .,' Renoir shook his head sadly, 'I know
it's a bad influence.'

Soon after this, attending a reception given in his honour
by the Calcutta Film Society, Renoir submitted himself to
a barrage of questions ranging from the most absurd to

the most abstruse, all of which he answered with great ease and candour in his charming broken English. Asked about *The River*, Renoir said that he had chanced upon a review of the novel in *The New Yorker*. The outline of the story, as *The New Yorker* gave it, had seemed to him to contain the elements of an interesting film. A reading of the novel had confirmed the impression, and Renoir had set about preparing a treatment.

I had not read the novel, and had no idea what the story was about, except that it had something to do with a river in Bengal (presumably the Ganges). But after all the nightmarish versions and perversions of India perpetrated by Hollywood, I was looking forward with real eagerness to the prospect of a great director tackling the Indian scene. It was therefore an acute disappointment to hear Renoir declare that *The River* was being made expressly for an American audience, that it contained only one Indian character—a servant in a European household, and that we were not to expect much in the way of authentic India in it. Of course the background would be authentic, since all the shooting was to be done on location in Calcutta. I could not help feeling that it was overdoing it a bit, coming all the way from California merely to get the topography right.

'What goes wrong with the great continental directors when they go to work in Hollywood?' was a question many of us had in mind but few had the temerity to ask. But when at last it did come, Renoir's eagerness to answer it surprised and relieved us. 'I'll tell you,' he said. 'I'll tell you what happens to them. It is the American mania for organisation which frustrates them. You have heard of this mania, of course, but you know nothing unless you have seen it in action. Suppose you are in the United States, and you want to go somewhere. So you go to a station to

catch a train. And what do you find? You find the train
arrives on time. Exactly on time. Now this is very strange.
In France the trains don't run on time. You are not used
to this punctuality, and it makes you feel uneasy. Then
you go to work in a studio. You are on the floor, ready to
begin work. And what do you find? You find you have to
go by the schedules, and so many of them. Which means
you are supposed to run on time, too. And then they begin
to check. They check the sound and doublecheck it, so that
you get perfect sound; they check and doublecheck the
lighting, so you get perfect lighting, which is also good.
But then they check and doublecheck the director's inspiration—which is not so good.'

Renoir feels that the best intentions are apt to be thwarted
in Hollywood owing to certain immutable factors. He
mentioned the star system, the endless codes of censorship
and the general tendency to regard films as a mass-produced
commodity as being the three most obvious. Once in a rare
while a director is lucky enough to find the right story, the
right sort of players (not stars) to act in it, and the right
sort of artistic freedom to make it, and the result is a worthwhile film. Only once, when he made *The Southerner*, was
Renoir able to work in such ideal conditions in Hollywood.

Renoir also believes that the best films of a country are
produced in times of stress; that an atmosphere of smug
self-complacence is bad for the cinema. 'Look what the war
has done to Italian films,' he said. 'Look at *Brief Encounter*.
I don't think a great film like that would have been
possible without all those air raids London had to suffer. I
think what Hollywood really needs is a good bombing.'

'Look at those flowers,' said Renoir, pointing at a *palas*

tree in full bloom. It was the first of several occasions on which I was fortunate enough to accompany him on his trips in search of locations. 'Those flowers,' said Renoir, 'are very beautiful. But you get flowers in America too. Poinsettias, for instance. They grow wild in California. But look at the clump of banana trees, and that green pond at its foot. You don't get that in California. That is Bengal.' One could see that while searching for locations, Renoir was also searching for *la couleur locale*, for those quintessential elements in the landscape which would be pictorially effective as well as being truly evocative of the atmosphere of the country. As he put it: 'You don't have to show many things in a film, but you have to be very careful to show only the right things.'

For a man of his age and dimensions, Renoir's enthusiasm and energy are phenomenal. He would trudge across miles of impossible territory to find the right viewpoint for the right locale. At times the absorption in his work was so complete that his wife would have to administer some gentle admonishment like: 'You shouldn't be out in the sun so long, Jean,' or 'Jean, you haven't forgotten that appointment at six o'clock, have you?'

During these trips Renoir spoke a great deal about himself. Of his youth; of his father, and the other great figures of the Impressionist movement; of ceramics—his other great passion besides the cinema; and of the cinema itself. It was during the First World War, while convalescing in a hospital from a leg wound, that Renoir had first toyed with the idea of a possible career in the cinema, although the actual apprenticeship was to come later, after he had gone through a spell of journalism. While he spoke in glowing terms of the *avant-garde* movement, Renoir characterised the entire silent period of the French commercial cinema as being largely stagnant and ineffectual. With the coming of sound, however, there was a sudden and magical transformation. As Renoir put it: 'It was as if someone had opened a secret door of communication between the film maker and his audience. It was a great feeling. Everything we did the audience understood. The French cinema could not have made those enormous strides towards maturity without this wonderfully perceptive audience. They helped us all along the way, and I for one feel grateful to them.'

The rich period lasted till the Occupation, after which, although there was no loss in technical quality—since the Germans were anxious to prove their munificence in regard to cultural activities—there was an inevitable falling off in content.

Of his early films Renoir spoke of *La Chienne* as being one of his favourites. 'It is a pity they had to remake it in Hollywood, and so badly,' he said. (This second version, directed by Fritz Lang, was called *Scarlet Street*.) Among the great masterpieces of the late thirties, Renoir had a special affection for *La Règle du Jeu* because it was entirely his own creation. He even acted a role in it. The case of *Partie de Campagne* was peculiar. It appears that Renoir had wanted to experiment with the short story film. For ease of commercial exploitation, two such short films would have to be made, and Renoir had started on the Maupassant story hoping to follow it up with a second one. But unfortunately the film had to be abandoned before it was quite finished. All through the Occupation the negatives lay hidden away by a friend to prevent destruction at the hands of the Nazis. It was only after the Liberation that prints were made and the film released with explanatory titles filling the gaps in the narrative.

Renoir himself had yet to see *Partie de Campagne*. For on

the very day the Germans had marched into Paris, Renoir
had marched out, taking with him his wife, and just such
of his worldly belongings as could be got into one small
suitcase.

From Paris to Hollywood. The inevitable trammels of
adjustment apart, Renoir had found life in California
pleasant enough. The climate was good, and there were
good friends. Chaplin—*le maître*—the mere mention of
whose name would make him beam, was one of the best.
Renoir was sorry for him. 'He is a sad man now,' he said.
'Nobody understands him in America.' I asked him if he
was aware of Chaplin's future plans. Renoir said: 'Well,
the last time I met him he was thinking of a musical in
which the characters would represent contemporary political figures. But I don't think he'll make it, because he also
seemed very anxious to displease nobody, and you can't
make a film like that and displease nobody.'

Of the five films he had made in Hollywood, Renoir
never mentioned *The Diary of a Chambermaid* or *Swamp
Water*. He had made *This Land Is Mine* as a rejoinder to
the notion then prevailing in America that the resistance
movement in Europe was a myth, and that every person
in an occupied country was a collaborator. *The Southerner*
he had enjoyed making mainly because it was a bit of
authentic America, and the people in it were real. He
considered it his best American film.

The Woman on the Beach was something of a misadven-
ture. Originally what interested Renoir in the story was
the character of the woman who 'lived only for love'.
But after he had begun to make the film, he had discovered to his chagrin that the Code prevented him from
developing the character in the way it needed to be dev-

eloped. As a result, in situations which called for a forth-
right emotional treatment, he had to fall back on sub-
terfuge and extraneous technical claptrap (hence the near-
surrealism of the setting, and the distracting dissonances
of the Hanns Eisler score).

To Renoir, there is nothing more important to a film
than the emotional integrity of the human relationship
it depicts. Technique is useful and necessary in so far as
it contributes towards this integrity. Beyond that it is
generally intrusive and exhibitionist. 'In America,' said
Renoir, 'they worry too much about technique, and neglect
the human aspect.'

I asked Renoir what he thought about the recent American trend towards documentary realism. 'That is nothing
new', he said. 'I shot most of *La Bête Humaine* on location
in Le Havre. I built very few sets for *The Southerner*. But
I am not dogmatic about it. I think a set is a useful and
necessary thing at times. And in any case, if the people
don't behave in a realistic manner there is no point in
having them perform against real backgrounds. I have
also heard theories about using non-professional actors.
This I don't understand at all. Can you think of a non-
actor replacing Raimu or Gabin? I can't. Personally,
I have a great respect for the acting profession.' For all
his vast experience, Renoir is surprisingly free from aesthetic dogmas. I think he summed up his attitude beautifully
when he said: 'Each time I make a new film, I want to
feel like a child who is learning about the cinema for the
first time.'

The day before he left for Europe, I saw Renoir again
in his hotel. He was taking with him a trunkful of memen-
toes, some of which he had picked up himself at bazaars
and curio shops. In the four weeks of his stay in Calcutta
he had travelled, and observed, and reflected. Bengal had

grown on him. The enchantment and novelty of the landscape on the one hand, and the picture of filth and misery
and poverty on the other. I had watched him go into ecsta-
sies over a simple hut, and pass into gloomy despondency
at the sight of a beggar. The visit to a coal mine had stirred
him so deeply that he said: 'If you could only shake Hollywood out of your system and evolve your own style, you
would be making great films here.'

He was to return to Calcutta with his unit in November,
which is the best time for shooting outdoors in India. Of
course the script had to be rewritten. 'This time, when I'm
in London, I must sit down with Rumer Godden and discuss the story. I may want to make some changes in it; add
a few characters, maybe. Maybe an Indian family to show
the contrast between their way of life and the foreigners'.
It would be a good idea. . . .'

As I came away from the hotel that evening I felt convinced that there was any amount of creative vigour still
left in Renoir. Perhaps *The River* would mark the beginning of a fresh and vital period after all the disappointments
of Hollywood. As he had now become an American citizen,
the chances of returning to Paris were somewhat remote.
The important thing, however, was to get away from the
synthetic environment of Hollywood and India was as
good a refuge as any. There is no doubt that here Renoir
would get his freedom. There would be no schedules
to distract him, and no checking and doublechecking of
inspiration. And of course, out here, the trains never will
run on time.

1949

Some Italian Films I have Seen ✍

I can do no more, within the scope of this bulletin, than touch on the most striking and significant aspects of the Italian films I had occasion to see abroad. A total assessment of the achievements of the neo-realist school is out of the question, as I had missed some of its most typical products—notably the films of Luigi Zampa, Pietro Germi, Mario Soldati, and the best films of Roberto Rossellini. However, the films that I did see afford a fair cross-section of present trends in the Italian cinema.

It was perhaps unfortunate that the first film to come my way should have been Vittorio de Sica's *Bicycle Thieves*. This film, which René Clair has called 'the best in thirty years', creates a norm which few films aspire to, let alone attain. Following upon it, Guiseppe de Santis's *Bitter Rice* seemed incurably blatant and vulgar. With the exception of *Stromboli*—which had, as Rossellini would insist, the sullying touch of Hollywood upon it—*Bitter Rice* is the only example of neo-realist cinema which the Indian public has had a chance to see. If it failed to create an impression on our intelligentsia, it is because, in spite of all his striving after documentary conviction, De Santis is essentially a second-rate artist preoccupied more with showmanship than with social problems. As a craftsman he is impressive enough, but not to be compared with, say, the Czech Otakar Vavra, whose similar mastery of the camera is always subservient to the functional demands of his narrative. De Santis's previous film *Caccia Tragica* (Tragic Pursuit) makes fewer errors of taste, but is even less successful in its attempted fusion of social tract and lurid melodrama.

Alberto Lattuada's films reveal a curious conflict of opposing tendencies: the iconoclast clashing with the traditionalist. In his *Senza Pietà* (Without Pity) one watches a daring and important theme—the love of a negro G.I. for an Italian girl—swamped by a needless profusion of plot and character. The same director's *Il Mulino Del Po* (The Mill on the Po)—one of the few instances of a neo-realist director's treatment of a period theme—is an altogether more impressive achievement. In depicting an agrarian revolt in the nineteenth century, Lattuada employs a studiedly grand style reminiscent of John Ford in its use of monumental close-ups and vast panoramic long shots. But the story itself lacks simplicity and strength of line, too many conflicting motivations clutter up the second half, and *Il Mulino*, for all its visual elegance, ends up a noble failure.

Neither De Santis nor Lattuada can be said to break away from convention as completely or as successfully as Renato Castellani. This young director's work has a wholly distinctive flavour. His style, which has no parallel in England or America, is marked by an astonishing verve and agility in the handling of plot, characters, and camera; a profusion of telling details, and sharp changes of mood and locale. It is a strikingly original narrative method. One has to keep a firm hold on one's wits to be able to grasp all the points Castellani makes with bewildering rapidity. Where the narrative itself lacks point and direction, as in *Sotto il Sole di Roma*, Castellani's fast pace begins to pall. One longs for some repose; the sharp contrasts begin to defeat their own emotional and aesthetic purpose and become merely decorative. But in his best film, *E' Primavera*, he achieves a wholly fascinating texture. Here one is never in doubt of Castellani's talent. One feels he has it, if anything, in excess.

If Castellani is concerned primarily with the volatile aspect of life, Luchino Visconti, in *La Terra Trema* (The Earth Trembles), depicts the slow decaying process of poverty and exploitation on a Sicilian fishing family. *La Terra Trema* was an obviously ambitious undertaking. Visconti shot the film entirely on location in a Sicilian village and selected his players from among the local inhabitants. In its original version, the film lasted well over three hours: the one I saw in London had been pared down to two, but had seemed like six. Had Visconti's talent been as far-reaching as his ambition, the film might have been a masterpiece. At it stands, *La Terra Trema* is a great bore, a colossal aesthetic blunder and a monumental confusion of styles. The grim naturalism of its locale is in constant conflict with the behaviour of its human beings—deliberate and stylised to the point of ballet. Visconti's meticulous composition within the frame heightens this feeling of artificiality. Moreover, in an effort to achieve a slow rhythm, he holds his shots till long after they have ceased to perform their expressive functions, and boredom results from a cumulation of a hundred such 'blank' moments when the audience is obliged to contemplate on the abstract qualities of images which were, however, not primarily intended for such contemplation. A slow pace is not in itself a bad thing. It is, in fact, as legitimate to films as it is to music or ballet or any other art that exists in time. But it needs a Bach to write a Sarabande that needs a Casals to do justice to it. The long, slow passages in the epics of Dreyer and Eisen-

stein are sustained only partially by their purely visual
qualities, rich and rewarding though they are: it is the
emotional conviction of these sequences, achieved through
precision of interpretation, of acting integrated to the
director's total stylistic approach, that is finally responsible
for their strength, their aesthetic 'rightness'. Had Visconti
realised—as the French director Georges Rouquier had
realised in his peasant documentary *Farrebique*—the limitations of using natural type players, and the importance of
emotional conviction, *La Terra Trema* would have been a
different film.

To Roberto Rossellini belongs the distinction of having
introduced the post-war Italian film to the world. Two
of his most important films, *Paisa* and *The Miracle*, eluded
me. I am therefore reluctant to make any except the most
generalised comments on him. His *Open City* does not
bear out all the claims that were made for it. The manner
of its making had been dramatised and publicised beyond
reason. After all, the basic requirements for film making
had been there, or else *Open City* would have remained
a concept in Rossellini's head. And, as Robert Flaherty has
demonstrated, if you have a camera that takes a film and
a film that takes pictures, all it takes besides to make a
masterpiece is Imagination. Some physical labour might
be involved, but such labour is not unknown in other
spheres of creative activity. In the end the process of creation is important only in so far as it directly influences
the work, in its form as well as in its content. Admittedly,
Open City derives some of its power from the anarchic social
condition in which it was made. But it seems certain that
the jagged contours of its narrative, its slapdash continuity,
are due less to lack of apparatus than to Rossellini's inherent incapacity for sustained constructive thinking. Perhaps
his talent is best displayed in the short stories of *Paisa*,

and the forty-minute *Miracle*. His formal indiscipline becomes a definite handicap to a film like *Open City* which
has otherwise a well constructed plot within the conventions of melodrama. Rossellini's handling of actors, too,
is perfunctory. The children in *Open City* behave in a dis-
concertingly adult fashion, and the best histrionic moments
in the film occur when seasoned professionals like Magnani
and Aldo Fabrizi take the stage. His dependence on professional acting takes an extreme form in *La Voce Umana*
(The Human Voice), a transcription of a Cocteau play
in which for full forty-five minutes Anna Magnani is the
only actress on the screen carrying on a one-sided conversation with her lover on the telephone, pleading with
him not to desert her. Every agony of the woman is caught
and sustained by Magnani through long continuous 'takes'.
But in the end, one is left with the uncomfortable feeling
that she could have gone through the same performance
in a drawing room (a stage would not afford the close-
up) for the benefit of friends, and with as much artistic
success.

As early as 1932, Mario Camerini's *Gli Uomini che Mas-
calzoni* (All Men Are Like That) revealed tendencies which
have now become common practice of the neo-realist
directors. *Gli Uomini* is a pleasing romantic comedy, distinguished from its contemporary Hollywood counterparts by the use of natural locales which lend conviction,
visual interest, and freedom of movement to the story.
Molti Sogni per le Strade (Many Dreams Along the Street)
which Camerini produced in 1948 is an extension of his
early style; only this time, the comedy is complicated and
refracted by social implications, so that, in the end, irony
prevails. *Molti Sogni* is the type of story in which a simple
initial situation gives rise to a chain of resultant situations
which the best Italian directors seem peculiarly gifted

to handle. Of this type, another example is Alessandro Blasetti's *Quattro Passi Fra Le Nuvole* (Four Steps in the Clouds) which was made in 1942 and is therefore, properly speaking, a pre-neo-realist product. It uses professional actors in a story which has for its hero a travelling salesman, a stolid individual with a nagging wife. On one of his journeys to the suburbs he chances to meet a young girl who, he discovers, is with child by a lover who has deserted her. Her problem: how could she in her present state face her conservative peasant family to which she was now returning? Circumstances, and a touch of pity, make the salesman decide to present himself to the family as the girl's husband. Some highly enjoyable farce results from this decision. The deception is successful for a while until it is discovered by the girl's father, the most conservative of the lot, and it is only through some inspired and highly persuasive reasoning by the hero that a major crisis is averted. After this, of course, things end happily for everyone—except for our salesman, who had meanwhile developed a genuine affection for the girl, but who is obliged to return reluctantly to the drabness of his henpecked, petit-bourgeois existence. *Quattro Passi* is the kind of plot that stands or falls by its treatment. In Blasetti's hands it becomes imbued with freshness and charm and bucolic humour.

Like Camerini and Blasetti, Vittorio de Sica is a veteran of the cinema. He started as an actor, became immensely popular in the thirties and continued to act even after taking to direction in 1940. His first three films have not been shown outside of Italy. The fourth, *I Bambini Ci Guardano* (The Children are Watching Us), is a contemporary of *Quattro Passi* and hence pre-neo-realist. Like Blasetti's film, it uses professional actors, but unlike it, there is scarcely a ray of sunshine in this grim and gripping

account of the disintegration of a middle class family
through marital disharmony. Everything is laid bare for
dissection—the strained relationship between husband and
wife, with a lover on the fringe; their separation; the wife's
passionate interludes with the lover; the final disruption
of the marriage; and the husband's ultimate suicide. And
to all this a witness—now dumb, now mystified, now
rebellious—their four-year-old son. *I Bambini Ci Guardano*
was a staggering revelation to those who had thought
De Sica's first considerable achievement was *Shoeshine*, produced in 1946. *Shoeshine* followed in the wake of *Open
City* and was accorded the same sort of reception, but with
greater justification. It uses the same technical equipment
as *Open City*, but contains none of the latter's clumsiness.
De Sica's superb handling of actors and unerring instinct
for expressive details circumvent such purely technical
drawbacks as fogged film-stock, inadequate processing and
imperfect post-synchronisation of dialogue. But although
De Sica's power of observation never deserts him, *Shoeshine*
is less rewarding as a work of art than either *I Bambini*,
or the masterpiece that followed it, the celebrated *Bicycle
Thieves*.

De Sica made *Bicycle Thieves* in 1948 from a script by
Cesare Zavattini. Subsequent films based on Zavattini's
stories confirm the impression that he is one of the best
writers for the cinema today. His greatest assets are an
acute understanding of human beings and an ability to devise the 'chain' type of story that fits perfectly into the
ninety-minute span of the average commercial cinema.
Simplicity of plot allows for intensive treatment, while a
whole series of interesting and believable situations and
characters sustains interest. *Bicycle Thieves* is the best example so far of such a story, perfectly translated to the
screen in the most universally comprehensible terms. Such

is its range of appeal that *Life* magazine at one extreme and Grigori Alexandrov writing in *Soviet Literature* at the other acclaim it equally as a masterpiece; while its long runs in England and America have made it one of the most popular films of recent times.

Basically, the theme of *Bicycle Thieves* is the classical one of chase, of hunt; in this case, for a stolen bicycle which stands between its owner and starvation. Like all basic film themes, this one could be treated and embellished in a hundred ways, depending on the director's approach to it. Zavattini's treatment makes room for pathos, humour and excitement, as well as digs at the police, the church, the brothel and phony astrology. It paints a sharp and poignant picture of a working class family; it depicts a father-and-son relationship that is among the subtlest and most profound in the cinema; it even manages to draw some sympathy for the bicycle thief; and finally, in its ultimate note of tragic gloom it seems to sum up, Verdoux-like, an entire epoch of despair and frustration.

Bicycle Thieves is a triumphant rediscovery of the fundamentals of cinema, and De Sica has openly acknowledged his debt to Chaplin. The simple universality of its theme, the effectiveness of its treatment, and the low cost of its production make it the ideal film for the Indian film maker to study. The present blind worship of technique emphasises the poverty of genuine inspiration among our directors. For a popular medium, the best kind of inspiration should derive from life and have its roots in it. No amount of technical polish can make up for artificiality of theme and dishonesty of treatment. The Indian film maker must turn to life, to reality. De Sica, and *not* De Mille, should be his ideal.

1951

Hollywood Then and Now ✐

One of my early childhood memories is of a man with a grin. He had rings in his ears and a bandanna around his head. He fought a band of fierce-looking men in big turbans, beat them all and jumped off a high parapet. Then he got up on a horse which took wings and flew away.... This was *The Thief of Bagdad*, and Douglas Fairbanks, Senior, was my first screen idol.

Then there was the man who never grinned at all. But he was terribly funny, and he did the same sort of acrobatic feats as Fairbanks. This was Buster Keaton. I saw him do a pole jump from a garden which took him sailing over the tree tops and through a third floor window and landed him, feet first, on the solar plexus of the villain.

Chaplin was another favourite, of course, with a face as malleable as Keaton's was frozen. It was difficult to imagine a time when Chaplin did not exist, or a time when he would not. Sydney was Chaplin's brother. He was the addled explorer who dressed up as a Scottish Highlander and prowled through dubious African jungles in search of dubious voodoo charms. Sydney wore spectacles without glasses. So did Harold Lloyd. But we did not question them, as later we did not question the painted moustache of Groucho Marx. So long as the laughs kept coming, we did not mind anything at all.

Sometimes there were tears and not laughter, and we did not mind that either. Chaplin was rare in making you cry in a funny film. Then, there were films which were sad films where you mostly cried. *Uncle Tom's Cabin,* for instance. I remember little Evangeline in her death-bed with the family gathered around in a tableau of sad resignation. As Eva breathed her last and we felt the lumps in our throats, an angel, transparent, complete with harp and flapping wings, rose out of her body and ascended towards the ceiling.

Other memories form an intriguing montage as I look back on my film-going in the twenties. Laughter and tears and thrills ... Lillian Gish, in the *Way Down East,* stepping precariously from one floating chunk of ice to another while fiendish bloodhounds nosed along her trail; John Gilbert, as the Count of Monte Cristo, delirious at the sight of gold in a treasure chest; Lon Chaney, as the Hunchback, clutching with dead hands the bell ropes of Notre Dame, and—perhaps the most exciting memory of all—the chariot race in *Ben Hur,* undimmed by a later and more resplendent version, for the simple reason that the new Messala is no match for the old and dearly hated one of Francis X. Bushman.

From the *Ben Hur* of 1925 to the *Ben Hur* of 1960, American films have come a long way, and then—as we shall find—gone back a little. But let us stick to the beginnings now. The feature film, as we know it, came about in the middle of the second decade. It was a product of Hollywood. In fact, we can narrow it down a lot more and say with perfect truth that it was the creation of one man, and one man alone. That man was D. W. Griffith. Griffith was born in Kentucky. In 1907, he gave up journalism, which he loved, to join films, which he loathed. He only hoped the new profession would bring him more money, but he was so ashamed of it that he took a false name. Seven years later, in 1914, he made *The Birth of a Nation*, which happened to be no less than the first full-fledged, large-scale demonstration of the potentialities of the film medium. Within a year of this, Griffith made *Intolerance*, an even more elaborate and ambitious work. If there is an instance of a similar event in the history of any other art, I am not aware of it. If the grammar of film making had to be studied, then *The Birth of a Nation* and *Intolerance* were the textbooks, and they were soon to be used as such by film makers all over the world. But Griffith himself—in a process as mysterious as his sudden emergence—began rapidly to decline and, by the end of the silent era, was a forgotten man.

His influence, however, had spread far and wide. By the twenties, films were being made in large numbers in France, Germany, Italy and Sweden. One began to hear more and more of a new breed of creative artists—the film directors. There were Murnau and Lubitsch and Lang in Germany, Gance and Feyder in France, Seastrom in Sweden, Pudovkin and Eisenstein in Russia.

The United States had a growing industry at home, but it lacked the prestige that continental films seemed to be winning. It is true that Griffith's films had won artistic success, and the great comedians had won fame and fortune. But this was not enough. There was a new audience —the post-war audience—with a new sophistication and new moral attitude, which was not pleased with the home product. So something had to be done.

The men who decided the turn of events at this point were the men who, for better or worse, ultimately shaped the movie industry in Hollywood. They were the entrepreneurs, the producers and studio owners—men like Zukor and Mayer, Goldwyn and Carl Laemmle, and what they did was to promptly set about importing big names from the European film world, no matter at what cost.

So Lubitsch came, and Seastrom and Murnau and Lang, and in time many more were to come. And not only directors, but actors and actresses, cameramen, set designers and all manner of other technical people were brought over and fitted into the scheme of things in Hollywood. Overnight, Hollywood found itself studded with new stars— Garbo, Pola Negri, Vilma Banky, Novarro, Valentino. From Germany and France came highly gifted cameramen like Karl Freund, Fritz Wagner and Rudolf Maté.

As for writers, there was a time when Sir James Barrie, Joseph Conrad, Arnold Bennett, Somerset Maugham, Robert Hichens and E. Phillips Oppenheim were all working in Hollywood, at the same time, and in the same studio.

No wonder the very texture of films began to change. The hearts-and-flowers sentimentality and the Victorian priggishness soon disappeared, and both style and content began to show signs of a sophistication that the new audience was quick to appreciate.

One of the first sound films I saw was by Lubitsch. It was called *Trouble in Paradise*. It opened with a moonlit shot of the romantic Grand Canal in Venice. The inevitable gondola appeared, glided up the glistening water, and, as it moved closer, turned out to be filled with garbage. The fat gondolier pulled up the boat in front of a villa, collected some more garbage and, at the point of rowing off, burst into an aria by Verdi.

Lubitsch was all wit and elegance and innuendo, and had a permanent influence on all future makers of sophisticated comedy. He was also one of the few topnotch European directors to survive and really succeed in Hollywood.

Others were less lucky. They persisted and fought the various pressures for a while, and then went back home gasping for breath.

One of the things about their employers that irked these directors was their conservatism. They loved to cling to safe formulas. Often the directors would be given stories which were nothing but reworkings of their own past successes. The Frenchman René Clair had strong feelings about this. It is said that when he left Hollywood his parting words to his employer were: 'Goodbye, 19th Century Fox.'

I do not wish to give the impression here that the producers were banking solely upon their European acquisitions. Importation of celebrities had been as much a fad as an economic necessity with Hollywood Moguls. And since the celebrities often brought something genuinely new and exotic with them, they usually paid good dividends. But the fact remains that there has never been a lack of local talent in Hollywood, even in the very early stages. Directors like Cecil B. De Mille and Thomas Ince were already active when Griffith made *Intolerance*, and one of Griffith's assistants, called Erich von Stroheim, made his mark as an exceptional film maker shortly after Griffith himself. Among others were Henry King, James Cruze and Rex Ingram—all students of Griffith and all learning the trade the hard way and working up towards independent assignments. In comedy, producers like Mack Sennett and Hal Roach were employing the best local talents and perfecting a style of slapstick that was uniquely American.

The coming of sound upset the jigsaw pattern of film making. But it had at least one immediate good effect. It gave films a boost which in turn helped the industry to survive the Depression.

From the technical and aesthetic points of view, sound created all manner of problems. Garbo, who was then the top star, was whispered to have a bad speaking voice. Chaplin did not want to talk at all. Sennett toyed with sound for a while and gave up. Keaton retired. The entire school of visual comedy found itself in jeopardy, and so did those among the exotic stars who found there was nothing they could do very quickly about their accents.

Hollywood now had no use for pantomime. What it needed were men and women who could, in addition to the camera, keep the microphone usefully engaged. Thus began a great influx of new talent into Hollywood. The newcomers fell into two broad groups: the talkers and the singers. The first were cast in plays—Broadway successes —and just talked. O'Neill's *Strange Interlude*, which I happened to see, had Norma Shearer and Clark Gable and the most ponderous weight of words that ever crushed a film. The second group—the singers—were just paraded across the screen and did their turns. I remember one such film in which Maurice Chevalier—just imported— turned up at small intervals with a new song each time. The rest was filled with Wheeler and Wolsey doing comic turns, Clara Bow and a crop of chorus girls doing whatever that drew whistles in those days, and a general display, rather like a fashion parade, of Paramount's roster of new stars.

If necessity were not the mother of invention, Hollywood could not have learnt to use sound as quickly and as effectively as it did. It was Lubitsch again who first showed that you could have a story, and you could have song, and you could weave the two so that you had a work of art.

The other thing you could do, it was found, was to have a story with a lot of action, and people them with

characters who would talk little if they talked at all. Thus
came the Westerns and the gangster films. In these, and
in the comedies that stemmed from Lubitsch, Hollywood
found her true métier.

Basically, both the Western and the gangster films were
films of violence. Good pitted against evil, battling for
supremacy, with crime failing to pay and law and order
restored in the end. In the Western, the setting and the
period gave the film a slightly remote, ballad-like quality.
The gangster films on the other hand had a harshness
and an immediacy which were wholly contemporary. The
genius of the best American directors lay in the handling
of this violence, which somehow transformed it and raised
it to a plane of poetry. In a John Ford Western—I think
it is *Fort Apache*—a platoon of cavalrymen under a foolish
and stubborn Henry Fonda faces an onslaught of Red
Indians and is wiped out in a matter of seconds. Men and
horses sprawl on the ground and a cloud of dust slowly
rises to conceal the pain and ignominy of defeat. Examples
of such poetisation of violence abound in the work of the
best American directors.

The conventions of the Western are almost as rigid as
those of, say, the classical sonata form in music. We recognise the lethal weapon twirled around the finger as we
recognise a trill or a turn in Mozart or Haydn. The barking
of unseen dogs as the stranger rides into town; the beer
jug slid along the counter; wine spouting out of bullet
holes in barrels; sage-brush rolling along windy wastes
of the prairie—these are all classic images of the Western.
It is true that in lesser hands they often turn into clichés,
but a master can use them time and again and yet preserve
their pristine freshness.

The conventions of the gangster film and its many
derivatives are perhaps less well defined, but here too there

are authentic images: cars careering round bends; bullets scarring windshields, pocking facades of buildings; the drooping wail of siren as the police arrive on the scene of the crime; the slouched hat and the crouching gait—all these we know as we know the turns of phrase in Hemingway and Chandler and Dashiell Hammett.

No less than the films of violence, the true American comedy, with or without music, is a thoroughly indigenous product. The purely visual comedy died with the last silent films of Chaplin. The purely verbal ones have no validity as films. So we are left with the ones that sought to combine the two. These, to be really good, had to fulfil three main conditions: they had to be well written, they had to be well directed, and they had to be well acted. Fortunately, Hollywood had talented people working in all three capacities. Among the directors, Frank Capra, Leo McCarey, George Stevens, Preston Sturges, Billy Wilder have all proved their mettle in comedies. If they had to share their contribution with some very efficient writers and some excellent casts of performers, they were still dominating enough to have left their hallmarks on their films. And this is no mean achievement, particularly in the context of Hollywood.

I hope I may be pardoned for forgetting the name of the gentlemen who directed the Marx Brothers. In fact, I am inclined to doubt if there were any. If a director's function is to marshall the forces and impose order and sanity on the proceedings, then, obviously, he has no business to be within a mile of the Marxes. The relationship of art to inspired nonsense has never been very clearly defined. In any case, it would seem a little irrelevant to talk of art in connection with, say, *A Night at the Opera*.

But I will say this, that if I were given the choice of one, and only one film, to take with me to that desert island, I would go for a Marx film without a moment's hesitation.

Like so many other comedians, the Marx Brothers liked to lace their antics with music. Harpo played the harp, Chico the piano, and I think I remember Groucho once singing a song which rhymed Lydia with encyclopaedia. But this is not to suggest that they ever made a true musical film. They did not. For that, we have to look elsewhere.

The view is a little blurred, for a milling crowd is raising the dust. There are Chopin and Brahms and Schubert and Schumann, itching to get out of those costumes. There are the exotic *prima donnas*, the glamorous conductors, the music hall comedians. There is the cute little girl with the dimples doing the tap dance. There are the purveyors of those fads—the Big Apple, the Mambo, the Jitterbug, the Rock 'n' Roll, the Twist. But never mind, they will not stay long, because they did not come to stay in the first place. And when they go away, the dust will settle and the view will clear, and there will emerge a lithe little man with a boyish charm and a top hat, at the drop of which he will do a dance to a tune by Kern or Berlin, and you will instantly pardon a thousand sins the movies have committed and bless them for being there.

Fred Astaire did not advance the art of film making. He only justified its right to exist. For a look at a real revolution, we have to take a long leap forward and come right down to the present and watch men like Stanley Donen and Jerome Robbins at work. These men are harnessing every resource of camera, sound, cutting and colour to create a new art form—the first genuine film ballets, American to the core.

If Hollywood had stuck to the things that it did best, we would have fewer complaints, and certainly more plea-

sure out of our film-going as a whole. But such was not to
be. Hollywood had its quirks, and its neuroses. Hollywood
had its Star System, which meant that you had to begin
with the star, and not with a creative urge. Hollywood had
its ambitions, which meant you had to have a Karamazoff
with fin tails and shock absorbers. And Hollywood had to
contend with TV, which meant everything had to grow
bigger and bigger until all that was intimate and delicate
and refined was crushed and smothered out of existence.

Four years ago, in the August of 1958, I visited Hollywood. As I drove downtown in a yellow cab on my first
day there, I could see that I had come to what must be the
oddest-looking city in the world. No two buildings looked
alike, and some—which turned out to be restaurants—did
not look like buildings at all. The street names were painted
on kerbstones, which meant that if you had to spot them
quickly, you had to be a reptile. The numbers of houses
often ran to four digits. One part of the town had artificial
canals and fake Italian villas and was called Venice.
Another looked like the French Riviera and had the same
sort of vegetation, artificially grown.

It took an hour's drive to reach my destination, which
was one of the major film studios. Its facade had the right
imposing look that one expected. Inside, one had a feeling
of desolation. Some of the personnel, I was told, were
working in Europe on co-productions. But that alone
could not account for all the empty sound stages. I had a
feeling of being inside some ancient mausoleum. Lights
and cranes and trolleys lay around and gathered dust. On
one stage, I noticed some activity. A TV feature was being
shot. I spotted Robert Young. He was playing the father
in a family series that I was told had a high rating.

The next day I was taken around the lot at the Paramount Studios. They had just built part of a town for a Western. *One-Eyed Jacks*, it was to be called. Marlon Brando was to play the lead and Stanley Kubrick was to direct. The set was perfection itself. At one end of a street they had put up a huge painted sky to block the view of some modern factory sheds. I remarked to my guide that the sky was so convincing that it had me fooled for a moment. He said it was not surprising because the painters had kept on at it until the crows began to knock their heads against it. Later that day, I met Stanley Kubrick. On the strength of his *Paths of Glory*, Kubrick had seemed to me to be one of the white hopes of the American cinema. He had first-rate technique, he had style and I had a feeling that he had also something to say. I asked him how he felt about his new assignment. Kubrick shook his head and said he had a hunch that Brando was going to resent being directed by a comparative newcomer. Soon after this I learnt that Kubrick had quit and Brando had taken over the job of directing himself.

At the Disney Studios they were making a live feature called *Shaggy Dog*. When I arrived, a scene was being rehearsed with the main actor Fred MacMurray, a couple of men playing press reporters, and a very large shaggy dog. There was also a middle-aged dwarf who hung around, and I wondered what his business was. When the time for lighting came, MacMurray and the two actors took their positions, but not the dog. Instead, they had the dwarf put on a dog skin, get down on all fours and stand in for the animal.

The general look of a Hollywood shooting crew at work is one of crisp, concerted efficiency. This was very much in evidence on Billy Wilder's set of *Some Like It Hot*. A notice outside the gate said No Visitors, and yet I found the sound stage filled with people. I learnt they were mostly members of the crew. These people do not all work at the same time. On the contrary, you may find that while some are working, others may just stand around and do nothing for long stretches of time. The fact is, it is a question of Unions, and it works more or less like this: if you belong, let us say, to the Union that works the trolley, you do not work unless to work the trolley. You do not even walk over and help the grip with the big load he is carrying. Your Union does not permit that. All you may do is stand around and wait until they call you to work the trolley. If they do not, you just stand—and earn your pay.

Of all the directors I met in Hollywood, Billy Wilder seemed the most volatile, and the most optimistic. It did not seem likely that his *élan* was caused solely by the proximity of Marilyn Monroe, although it might have been one of the contributory factors. Most of the other directors I met had spoken of worries. George Stevens was worried about the wide screen; he was making *The Diary of Anne Frank* then. Kazan, in New York, had spoken of the lack of freedom in Hollywood and said he preferred to work in New York. But Wilder did not seem to have any worries at all. The first thing he said to me was: 'You won a prize at Cannes? Well, I guess you're an artist. But I'm not. I'm just a commercial man, and I like it that way.' I mumbled a word of protest and said I thought he was rather good at mixing art and commerce, and that two of his own films had won prizes at festivals in the past. But Wilder would have none of it. He just smiled and said: 'Watch Lemmon do this scene. He's great'— and walked off.

Thinking back on Wilder's remark now, I begin to see the truth that it contained. If you have real talent, and have found a break in Hollywood, and wish to keep going,

it may be best not to talk about Art too much. What you
have to try and do is keep your finger on the pulse of the
public, your wits about you, and keep working. This is
not easy but it has been done. If you are a success, they
will probably heed you, and may even give you your head.
And when they do that, you have your big chance. And if
you still have your head in the right place, and care enough
about Art, you may yet come out with something true
and strong and valid.

But this is rare in Hollywood, and we have known it
to be so for a long time. Once in a long while we've had
a *Grapes of Wrath*, a *Marty*, an *Ace in the Hole*, a *Sierra Madre*,
a *Little Foxes*, and we've been grateful for them. Even
today, the average standard of American films—for reasons
of sheer technical polish—is probably higher than anywhere else in the world. But the great film, the truly personal film, the film that is shaped and coloured by one
man's vision and feeling and sympathies, is rare if not
altogether extinct.

And there is little hope of an immediate revolution.
Twenty years ago, in Hollywood, a young man named
Orson Welles had a couple of bold flings at unconventional film making. In this he was only trying to do what
had already been done in the other arts. Painting and
music had been freed from the bondage of perspective and
tonality. Writers had been experimenting with words and
syntax and narrative styles. Welles gave expression to an
urge that was essentially contemporary. Yet Welles failed
to survive as an artist. *Citizen Kane* and *Magnificent Ambersons* had both had an oblique influence on future
film makers, but Welles himself had to go into exile in
Europe.

On my last day in Hollywood I went to the MGM
Studios and had lunch with an executive in the studio's

basement cafeteria. The place was packed with a weird collection of 'types'. I was told they were bit players—some with work and some idle. I was surprised to find, upon closer inspection, that I knew most of the faces from my early film-going days, and they were not all bit players then. One, Henry Wilcoxon, I remembered fighting the Crusades under De Mille.

As I pondered over the transient nature of the film profession, my host tapped me over the wrist and said he had a wonderful plan. He was going to produce a film about a great Indian; in fact, he had been thinking about it for a long time.

He said this with an earnestness that I found disconcerting. I remembered Ramon Novarro as Karim, the son of a Brahmin who wore the sacred thread *and* a Sikh turban; and I remembered Banerji, the westernised Hindu in *The Rains Came*, performing cabalistic rituals to appease the Rain God.

'Which great Indian?' I asked.

'The Lord Buddha,' he said. 'Light must come from the East, you know.'

I said: 'That's fine, but who're you going to cast in the lead?'

'Guess who,' said the Executive.

I made a quick mental survey of all the Oriental faces available to Hollywood, and could not think of one that filled the bill.

I said I could not guess.

The eyes of my host now gleamed with what I took to be a sneak preview of the light to come.

'Why,' he said, 'Robert Taylor, of course!'

1962

Thoughts on the British Cinema ✍

In the nineteen-thirties there used to be two cinemas next to each other in the heart of Calcutta's theatreland. The first one, as you came up the side street that contained them, showed only British films, while the other specialised in the American product. I was at school then and had already become something of a film addict. On Saturday afternoons I used to turn in at the side street and make a beeline for the second cinema, casting a contemptuous sidelong glance at the first one *en route*.

We did not think much of British films at the time. Word had got round over the years that the art of film making had somehow eluded the British. Sometimes, in a charitable mood, we modified this statement and said that the art of the British film eluded all but the British. At any rate, we were happy because we made films in Bengal and made them badly too. But then we were so far from the hub of things, and the cinema was after all an essentially western art form; no wonder we got a vicarious pleasure out of putting British films on a level of ineptitude with our own.

Not that we did not see British films at all. There were times when it turned out that the cinema showing American films was sold out, and we drifted to the other one and sat through the antics of Jack Hulbert and Gordon Harker, Gracie Fields and Jessie Matthews. These were comedies, mainly musical comedies, comedy thrillers and the like, but there was a marked difference between these and the comedies from Hollywood, which we enjoyed—the madness of the early Marx brothers as well as the more orderly humour of early Capra and Leo MacCarey. These American comedies, in order to be enjoyed, generally demanded no more than a sense of humour, a set of ribs to be tickled. For the British ones, too, you needed a sense of humour, but of a very exclusive, *British* sort. We laughed at Jack Hulbert not mainly because we were tickled, but because we did not want our British neighbours in the theatre to think that we had no sense of humour.

Today, thirty years later, we feel nostalgic about the American comedies of the thirties. I do not think there is a similar nostalgia, even amongst the British, for the films of Hulbert and Harker and Tom Walls. They were the dodos of British cinema, although we will say this much for them, that they did valiant service at a time when the British film makers knew only one way to sustain the film-goer's interest in the medium—by using personalities who could best put the audience in a state of uncritical acceptance.

Happily, however, the state of things has changed, and British films have come a long way from Music Hall comedies. The few films of the thirties that have left their mark on history had little to do with the National British cinema. They were films like *Rembrandt* and *The Private Life of Henry the Eighth*, made by the Hungarian Alexander Korda with a predominantly continental technical crew; the delightful comic fantasy *The Ghost Goes West*, made by the great French director, René Clair, with a mixed English and American cast; the films of Hitchcock like *Blackmail*, *The Lodger* and *The Lady Vanishes*, which by

their very nature could not be profound social documents;
and the *Pygmalion* of Anthony Asquith, which by being the
first Shaw film was in any case an exception. Only two or
three films of this period, such as *Bank Holiday* and *South
Riding*, bore hints of the social awareness that was to mark
the films of later periods.

The main stumbling block in the path of the British
film makers was, one suspects, the very fact of their being
British. I do not think the British are temperamentally
equipped to make the best use of the movie camera. The
camera forces one to face facts, to probe, to reveal, to get
close to people and things; while the British nature in-
clines to the opposite: to stay aloof, to cloak harsh truths
with innuendoes. You cannot make great films if you
suffer from constricting inhibitions of this sort. What is
more, the placidity and monotony of habit patterns that
mark the British way of life are the exact opposite of what
constitutes real meat for the cinema. The cinema revels
in contrasts, in clashes—however small and subtle. The
calm has to be ruffled, the patterns disturbed and tensions
created—and these have to be revealed in audible speech
and visible action, to provide the basic raw material for
the director to work upon. These were lacking in the
British scene. Or if they existed, then the creative imagination and daring to turn them into the stuff of cinema was
lacking. Hence the profusion of innocuous comedies and
musicals in the early period.

But if the British lacked the ability to create, they were
certainly not lacking in the power of appreciation of the
film as an art form. The film society movement grew and
spread quickest in Britain. The grammar of film making
was studied assiduously as an end in itself. The visit of
Sergei Eisenstein to England in 1930 was a momentous
occasion, and the young men who sat at his feet, men like

Basil Wright, Paul Rotha, Thorold Dickinson, Anthony Asquith and John Grierson, were later to come to the forefront of the British film scene.

The development of the documentary movement in Britain, headed by John Grierson, was surely a direct result of the influence of Soviet cinema in general and of Eisenstein in particular. But the films deriving from this impulse—documentaries like *Night Mail*, *Drifters*, *Song of Ceylon*, were far more typically products of the British imagination than the feature films of the same period.

One possible reason why the British took to documentaries was that it involved a legitimate process of dehumanisation and afforded opportunities for formal experiments which the theory-conscious British directors found exciting. These documentaries enjoyed the collaboration of the best literary and musical talents in Britain, and they live today more as works of art than as social documents.

It was the Second World War which really forced the British film makers to come out of their shells and speak with both their minds and hearts through their films. As Jean Renoir once remarked, the Battle of Britain, through destruction of life and property, was wholly beneficial to the British film industry.

The war ruffled the calm, disturbed the pattern and created the tensions. Britain had not been lacking in craftsmanship; to this was now added an urge to say something and say it quickly and well. The whole social scene was bristling with the stuff of cinema. The creative imagination, constricted so long, was suddenly set free.

Not all the good films made in the war years dealt with the topic of war. There were films of novels, such as *Kipps* from Wells, and *Stars Look Down* from Cronin; there were biographies like *The Prime Minister*, there was *The Rake's Progress* inspired by the famous series of paintings by Hogarth. But the most important film of this period was certainly David Lean's version of Noel Coward's one-act play *Brief Encounter*. *Brief Encounter* was a landmark for both what it said and the way it said it. It had a remarkable quality of freshness deriving from Lean's extraordinarily fluid and filmic treatment of what was essentially a very intimate and introspective subject, and from the poignant acting of two leading players, Celia Johnson and Trevor Howard. Above all, it was a film that was British to the core.

I am not sure how *Brief Encounter* would stand up to a reappraisal in the context of present-day film making; the texture of films has changed considerably in the last twenty years. In spite of occasional borrowings from such *avant-garde* works as Welles's *Citizen Kane*, *Brief Encounter* employed an essentially academic method of storytelling, observing the unities, employing judicious dramatic contrasts and variations of pace. In fact, a basically academic approach marked by a deep respect for the postulates of the theorists was a distinguishing feature of the British films of this period. By saying this I am not belittling them; I am merely specifying their characteristics.

Lean with *Brief Encounter* and *This Happy Breed*, Carol Reed with *The Way Ahead* and *Kipps*, Thorold Dickinson with *The Prime Minister*, Michael Powell with *Colonel Blimp*, Launder and Gilliat with *The Rake's Progress* and Asquith with *Fanny By Gaslight*—all gave the British cinema an unmistakable air of an artistic renaissance, and one waited with bated breath to see how it would shape and grow and how long it would last.

For some years at least, things looked good. There were powerful men at the helm—men like J. Arthur Rank and Michael Balcon who charted the course of things with smoothness, and were wise enough at the same time not to interfere too much with the directors, who thus enjoyed both affluence and artistic freedom.

Lean and Reed went from triumph to triumph. *Great Expectations*, which Lean produced in 1949, was and still remains the best Dickens film ever made. He followed this up with *Oliver Twist*, a colder film but with a truly astonishing craftsmanship. Reed made *Odd Man Out*, which fell only a little short of the dizzy height to which it aspired. Asquith, Dickinson, Launder and Gilliat, Powell and Pressburger all followed up their wartime successes with promising films.

About this time Reed said something very significant in a press interview. He was asked if he had any predilection for a particular type of subject, and he said that he would make any subject that came his way provided it could make a good script. This was by way of being a confession that Reed considered himself primarily to be a craftsman, that he did not have anything very special to say, and that he made films mainly for the love of the medium.

It was not long before one found out—not without a feeling of dismay—that this attitude of Reed's held good for most of the other important British directors. They had very little of their own to say, although they had any amount of competence and enthusiasm to convey other people's ideas through their films.

The true stature of these directors was revealed within a period of five or six years, and one knew that the renaissance had come to an end. The end of the forties saw the gradual disintegration of what was just beginning to be called a British National Style. Lean went more and more for surface polish, Reed abandoned the English social scene and went off on jaunty excursions into the Graham Greene world. There is little that was specifically British about the *Fallen Idol* and *The Third Man*, although there was much to admire deeply in both from a purely filmic point of view.

The same holds true of most of the other directors. Powell and Pressburger quickly established themselves as sumptuous entertainers. *Black Narcissus* had the incredible ingredients of Deborah Kerr as a nun in a convent in Darjeeling, Sabu as an Indian prince, Jean Simmons as a Nepalese dancing girl, and a Buddhist monastery which used both Ajanta-like murals and authentic marble traceries *à la* Mogul.

The others made competent but ephemeral films most of which were characterised by a high degree of technical polish but were almost totally devoid of the personal vision of genuine artists.

The fifties were marked by two dominant phenomena. Firstly, there was the emergence of a new school of British comedy, essentially filmic and therefore wholly distinct from the comedies of the thirties. Secondly, there was the emergence of Laurence Olivier as an interpreter of Shakespeare.

It is often difficult to locate the root cause of the emergence of a new trend in film making, but one thing is certain: a formula that pays at the box office tends to persist and flourish until the same box office spells its doom. It is true that the comedies of the fifties caught on and persisted, but an additional cause in the present case must have been the emergence of a comedian of quite outstanding calibre—a man able to play six different parts in the same film, each with equal conviction—one being that of a woman. *Lavender Hill Mob, The Man in the White Suit, Kind Hearts and Coronets* were all made to exploit the virtuosity of Alec Guinness; and of the several writers who fed this protean talent with suitably varied parts, the name of T. E. B. Clarke must head the list. Clarke was unique in that he was one of the few genuine screen writers in England who wrote specifically for the cinema.

Olivier's debut as director in *Henry V* in the late forties has been regarded, and rightly, as one of the most auspicious things to happen in the history of the British cinema. Olivier's films—he made three from Shakespeare—are marked by a dual anxiety to be faithful both to Shakespeare and to the aesthetic demands of the film medium. The method has its obvious pitfalls. Words are all-important to Shakespeare, and yet words have a constricting effect on movement. Right from *Henry V* through *Hamlet* to *Richard III*, Olivier's has been a series of grapplings with problems of static speech in a medium that wants to be mobile in order not to loosen its grip on the audience. Time and again Olivier has betrayed his anxiety in the very process of overcoming this problem. This has amounted to serious aesthetic flaws in otherwise magnificent works and has on the whole prevented him from achieving the highest eminence as a creative film maker.

Apart from the success of the comedies and of Olivier's Shakespeare films, the main feature that marked the fifties in Britain was the migration of the best British directors to Hollywood and the gradual disintegration of the others that stayed back. Hollywood considers polish to be the prime virtue of a film maker, and the first of the British directors to be lured away by the Movie Moguls was Alfred Hitchcock. Lean and Reed followed shortly after, and they were followed in their turn by Alexander Macken-drick, who made a fine comedy called *Whisky Galore*, and a young director called Michael Anderson who had made quite a promising debut with *Dam Busters*. The older of the documentary makers, like Harry Watt and Paul Rotha, gradually declined into inactivity. Dickinson took up a position supervising United Nations documentaries, and Humphrey Jennings, who had emerged in the war period and had the rare double qualification of being a craftsman as well as a thinker, died a premature death. It seemed for a time that the British cinema had reached its nadir of unproductivity.

But here and now some new stirrings were felt. The pattern was breaking again, the surface was being ruffled; and the tension this time was being created not by outside forces but by elements in the industry itself. New voices, voices of protest, were being heard. The time had come for a fresh resurgence, and it came hand in hand with a resurgence in the literary field. The renaissance of the sixties, at its height at the moment of writing this survey, was a direct offshoot of the literary movement created by the now celebrated Angry Young Men—a set of talented writers with working class backgrounds—John Osborne, John Braine, Allan Sillitoe, and a few others.

This new trend has a clear pattern and one dominant theme—class distinctions and the clash resulting from them. A dramatic theme, filmic and intensely British. One expects the trend to have a long and healthy existence. The por-tents have all been good. A whole new set of directors, writers and actors have come to the fore, and there has been the closest collaboration between them. In most cases this new and young group of directors—Karel Reisz, Tony Richardson, Lindsay Anderson, Jack Clayton—have revealed not only technical competence, but a genuine involvement in the social implications of these themes. They are all craftsmen as well as artists with visions and strong personal beliefs. As ever in Britain, they have been helped by their training in documentary; but as never before, they are not afraid to face facts and get close to people and things, and to probe with their minds and their hearts and their cameras. Britain, it seems, has at last a genuinely national school of film making and I, personally, can say with truth that I look forward now to films from Britain as much as to films from any other country.

1963

Calm Without, Fire Within ✍

As students of painting in Rabindranath Tagore's university in Santiniketan, we had to learn the rudiments of Chinese calligraphy. We rubbed our sticks of Chinese ink on porcelain palettes, dipped our bamboo-stemmed Japanese brushes in it and held them poised perpendicularly over mounted sheets of Nepalese parchment. 'Now draw a tree,' our Professor Bose would say (Bose was a famous Bengali painter who made pilgrimages to China and Japan). 'Draw a tree, but not in the western fashion. Not from the top downwards. A tree grows up, not down. The strokes must be from the base upwards . . .'

This was basic—this reverence for life, for organic growth. While you paint, each stroke of brush, each movement of finger, of wrist, of elbow, contemplates and celebrates this growth. And not just things that live and grow. Everything that comprises perceptible reality is observed, felt, analysed and reduced to its basic form, basic texture, basic rhythm.

Yet this convention is no straitjacket, for it has as its basis not mathematics, but Man. That is why one can distinguish a Harunobu woman from an Utamaro one, a Ma Yuan landscape from one by Li T'ang. Ultimately it is the personality of the artist that colours and shapes the work of art.

When we come to films, the pinning down of national traits becomes more difficult. For one thing, the distinguishing mark of the tool is absent. The brush and the burin have given way to the more impersonal and mechanical movie camera whose lenses are found to behave in a very occidental fashion, recording perspective and shadows in defiance of ageless precepts of Oriental Art. A landscape-with-figures in a Japanese movie—if one ignores the kimonos, the bamboo shoots and what not—is more likely to be found to obey the compositional canons of western academic art than those of the East—and rightly, too.

Where, then, does one look for the special eastern traits?

Perhaps it would be convenient if film makers of the East were occasionally to film western subjects in western settings. Jean Renoir made *The Southerner* in the United States and *The River* in India. To me they were more clearly revealing of his essential 'Frenchness' than his French films, and this as much in the handling of the human relationships (Renoir the Man) as in all that constituted the films' aesthetic substance (Renoir the Artist). But no such luck with the Japanese, who have to be judged on the basis of Japanese subjects. Even Akira Kurosawa's occasional forays into European classics have brought forth adaptations: Macbeth turned into a medieval Japanese warlord, and so forth.

All this has not prevented western critics from passing learned judgment on Japanese film makers, who have been extolled, castigated and categorised. Now, with silent films, this would not be an improper thing to do: after all, mime does have a quality of universality. But with speech added, and all that goes with it, this becomes a chancy thing unless one happens to be a specialist. The fact that screen format and tools of production are more or less standardised does not mean that a greater affinity exists between the films of the East and the West than in

other branches of art. On the contrary, films, being only
partially an abstract art, acquire colour from all manner of
indigenous factors such as habits of speech and behaviour,
deep-seated social practices, past traditions, present influences and so on. The more perceptive the film maker, the
more acutely is he aware of these factors and the better
able to weave them into the fabric of his work. How much
of this can a foreigner—with no more than a cursory knowledge of the factors involved—feel and respond to?

Take the question of language. In a sound film, words
are expected to perform not only a narrative but a plastic
function. A poor actor will stress words wrongly, miss
nuances, make errors of intonation. All this will be missed
unless one knows the language, and knows it well.

It is true that there are certain basic similarities in
human behaviour all over the world. Expressions of joy
and sorrow, love and hate, anger, surprise and fear, are fun-
damentally the same. But even these can exhibit minute
local variations which can only puzzle and perturb—and
consequently warp the judgment of—the uninitiated foreigner. And when a director essays a heightened style derived from some local dramatic tradition, it is futile to apply
any standards of judgment except those that relate to that
particular tradition.

Talking of social practices, I know of a western critic
who went to see my film *Pather Panchali* and was so upset
by the spectacle of Indians eating with their fingers that
he had to leave as soon as the second dinner episode commenced.

If all this sounds dampening for the critic let me assert
clearly that if total assessment is impossible, there still remains much that a good film from any source can offer to
the perceptive and sympathetic viewer.

I saw *Rashomon* in Calcutta soon after its triumph in Venice. This is the point where I should confess that my knowledge of the Far East is derived largely from Waley and Lafcadio Hearn; and that while I know my Shakespeare and my Schopenhauer, I have yet to know Murasaki and the precepts of Lao-tzu. At the turn of the century, a Japanese nobleman-aesthete, called Count Okakura, came to India to spread the gospel that Asia is One; linked, he said, by the same guiding principles of art and philosophy. Very well. But the fact remains that the Far East is content with only five notes in music while we in India have to have the full chromatic scale, with some quarter tones thrown in (I, personally, have to have my Bach and Mozart too). And if I love Chinese painting and Japanese woodcuts, it is not at the expense of my admiration for Cézanne and Piero della Francesca. And consider eating habits; the Chinese do not round off their meals with dessert, while we follow a Sanskrit proverb which says 'All meals must end with sweets.'

Disparities notwithstanding, the triumph of *Rashomon* was exciting. After all, was not the Lord Buddha born in India? And in any case it was time some sort of a challenge to western domination in films came from this part of the world.

And what a challenge it turned out to be. There was no doubt the Japanese had made a wily choice in selecting Kurosawa's film. I doubt if the work of other directors, like Kenji Mizoguchi or Yasujiro Ozu, would have made the same impact in the same circumstances. Here was a film masterful in technique and adult in theme and with just the right degree of universality to prevent alienation while retaining the pull of the exotic.

It was also the kind of film that immediately suggests

a culmination, a fruition, rather than a beginning. You could not—as a film making nation—have a *Rashomon* and nothing to show before it. A high order of imagination may be met with in a beginner, but the virtuoso use of cutting and camera was of a sort that came only with experience.

Later revelation of Kurosawa's past work and the work of other Japanese directors has confirmed what *Rashomon* hinted at: the existence of an art form, western in origin, but transplanted and taking root in a new soil. The tools are the same, but the methods and attitudes in the best and most characteristic work are distinct and indigenous. And much of this work suggests that the tenets of western theorists apply only to certain western forms of the cinema and must be modified if they are to be valid for both East and West.

Of all the Japanese directors, Kurosawa has been the most accessible to the outside world. There are obvious reasons for this. He seems, for instance, to have a preference for simple, universal situations over narrowly regional ones: the fear of nuclear destruction, graft in high places, the dehumanising effect of bureaucracy, simple conflicts of good and evil, the moral allegory in *Rashomon* and so on.

But most importantly, I think, it is his penchant for movement, for physical action, which has won him so many admirers in the West. 'Movies must move' is a dictum which has found its way into many a book of film aesthetics. I suspect it once had an appendage which has dropped off, like a lizard's tail: 'Movies must move, or else the audience will grow restive and leave in the middle' —or something like that. At any rate, these three words have acquired the sanctity of a commandment, and movement has been erroneously equated with physical action and such action extolled for its own sake.

I do not know Japan well enough to know if the Kurosawa brand of action is within the Japanese artistic tradition, or whether the director has a strong Occidental
streak in him. One way or the other, it does not very
much matter, so long as I am able to derive keen aesthetic
pleasure from a well-devised scene of battle or sword-
play.

If Kurosawa's affinities are in doubt, there is no doubt
that he is a man of vastly different temperament from
Ozu or Mizoguchi, both of whom come nearer to my pre-
conception of the true Japanese film maker. Here, too,
I may be wrong, but a phrase of my dear old professor
sticks in my mind: 'Consider the Fujiyama,' he would say;
'fire within and calm without. There is the symbol of the
true Oriental artist.'

Mizoguchi and Ozu both suggest enormous reserves of
power and feeling which never spill over into emotional
displays. And both directors seem almost anachronistic
in their apparent unawareness of western conventions.
But this only goes to prove that cinema is only what you
make of it and how you use it, and not what some hasty
pedagogue thinks it ought to be.

I am not saying that these masters did not learn from
the West. All artists imbibe, consciously or unconsciously,
the lessons of past masters. But when a film maker's roots
are strong, and when tradition is a living reality, outside
influences are bound to dwindle and disappear and a true
indigenous style evolve.

Another fact that strikes an outsider is that most of
these great Japanese directors seem to have worked un-
trammelled by considerations of popular reaction. Or else
Japan must have an unusually large public ready to back
serious artistic efforts. Toshiro Mifune, the actor, once
told me that the Japanese like their films long and heavy.

This must be partly true, because it is difficult to envisage a situation where a film maker can totally ignore the economic aspects of production, and keep on doing so for any length of time.

As an Indian film maker, I find there is a lot to admire greatly in Japanese movies. Perhaps there is some truth in Okakura's gospel, and there are more affinities than show on the surface.

I am struck by the search for inner truth that marks the best Japanese movies, as it marks their other arts. On a human level, the director reveals this truth through the medium of some of the best actors in the world today. Mifune, Tanaka, Mori, Machiko Kyo—these and others have a range that takes in the subtlest underplaying as well as the most bravura displays of emotion.

The quality of acting suggests a thoroughness and discipline that marks every aspect of film making, as it marks all Japanese art in general. I can imagine the Japanese sensibility recoiling from, say, the arbitrary, rough-cut quality of a film by Jean-Luc Godard. The true Japanese artist will tell you that a work of art must be healthy; it must live and breathe, inhale and exhale. What good is a film that stumbles and totters like a sick and maimed being?

Then there is the Japanese use of camera, of light. Light is used as the brush is by the painter—to feel and reveal the texture of things, to capture moods, to lend the right expressive weight to a given image. It is not as if expiessive photography has not been done in the West; only there has been less and less of it (until very recently) since the days of the silent cinema, when even a two-reeler could be invested with a subtle quality of truth, and when Stroheim pulled down the walls of apartment houses to let the light in for his shots. Hollywood, in particular, has shown a steady decline in its photography over the years. Highly paid simulators of nature and an ever-increasing battery of artificial lights have slowly displaced nature, with the result that cameramen have had to fall back for inspiration on such second-hand sources as academic painting and lush 'salon' photography.

It is perhaps the absence of a naturalist tradition in the visual arts in Japan that instils this reverence for natural light. The film maker is ever aware of its expressive power, and he knows the fine distinction between theatricality and legitimate cinematic devices. Think of Orson Welles's *Macbeth*, stumbling through eternal gloom amidst the simulated rocks and caves of the Republic sound stage; and of Kurosawa's Macbeth (in *Throne of Blood*) brooding on the heights of the Fujiyama. Real rain and mist and chilly wind charge the film with a conviction and poetry no studio can ever capture.

The Japanese know that it is the easiest thing for the movie camera to create tricks and illusions, and they have the innate sensibility to realize that such illusions, being obvious mechanical devices, can never have the suggestive power of actual hallucinations. That is why they invest even their ghosts with solidity. One has only to see Mizoguchi's *Ugetsu* to see that it works as no double printing has ever worked.

The complaint is frequently heard that some Japanese films—even some of the very good ones—are 'nevertheless very slow'. Some of my own films, too, have drawn this comment from western critics. Now, a slow pace is, I believe, as legitimate to films as it is to music. But as a director I know that a slow pace is also terribly hard to sustain. When the failure is the director's fault, he should be prepared to take the blame for it. But it is important to remember that slowness is a relative thing, depending on the degree of involvement of the viewer. And this degree is determined partly by the viewer's familiarity and sympathy with the various socio-aesthetic elements that go to make the film. We really come back to the question of the true connoisseur's response as opposed to the uninitiated layman's.

I have felt this again and again, reading the western critics on my own work. I am grateful to many of them for a lot of sympathy and understanding, as also, at times, for a degree of penetration that I would not have thought possible for a westerner. The stumbling block has mainly been, I suspect, the occasional unfamiliar, indigenous elements.

This is something I cannot help. I cannot even begin to elucidate, through films or in writing, the complexity of the people that inhabit my films. I concentrate on one —the Bengalis, of which I am one—out of a possible score or so, each with a different topography, dress, habits, tongue, physiognomy and even philosophy. Asia may be one, but India is by no means so.

Take a single province: Bengal. Or, better still, take the city of Calcutta, where I live and work. Accents here vary between one neighbourhood and another. Every educated Bengali peppers his native speech with a sprinkling of English words and phrases. Dress is not standardised. Although women generally prefer the sari, men wear clothes which reflect the style of the thirteenth century or conform to the directives of the latest *Esquire*. The contrast between the rich and the poor is proverbial. Teenagers do the Twist and drink Coke, while the devout Brahmin takes his daily dip in the Ganges and chants his *mantras* to the rising sun. . . .

What should you put in your films? What can you leave out? Would you leave the city behind and go to the village

where cows graze in the endless fields and the shepherd
plays his flute? You could make a film here that would
be pure and fresh and have the flowing rhythm of a boat-
man's song.

Or would you rather go back in time—way back to
the Epics, when the gods and the demons took sides in the
great battle where brother killed brother and Lord Krishna
revivified a disconsolate prince with the words of the *Gita*?
One could do exciting things here, using the great mimetic
tradition of the *Kathakali*, as the Japanese use their Noh
and Kabuki.

Or would you rather stay where you are, right in the
present, in the heart of this monstrous, teeming, bewildering city, and try to orchestrate its dizzying contrasts of
sight and sound and milieu?

Indeed, it could all be very exciting. But would the
public think it so?

And if they did not, could you afford to ignore them—
this semi-literate multitude that has been fed for years on
the tawdry and the false—and turn to the audience abroad?
But why should the West care? I am not sure I have all
the answers.

But I can at least keep guessing while I make my next
film, and the one after that . . .

1963

Moscow Musings 🖋

The morning was clear and sunny but it had started to
drizzle when we got off the bus in the compound of the
Mosfilm Studios—a good thirty miles from the centre
of the town. The film workers stood at the entrance to
the main building, and the look of concern in their faces
was obvious. 'We are sorry,' said a big man, coming forward. 'We had planned to make the speeches here, out in
the open, near the flower beds. Now we have to rush inside.'

We were herded into the lobby, nearly two hundred
of us, and found ourselves chock-a-block in a space barely
as large as a badminton court. A speech began, and I
moved over to the wall to look at the stills from films under
production.

Half an hour later we were driven to the sound stages
in an odd sort of glass-topped conveyance which had a
main car in front and two others hitched behind, and
we sat in rows facing each other. The Mosfilm compound
is large, and the shooting floors—seventeen of them—
are right at the back, ranged in two rows forming an L.
We were sorry to hear that no shooting was going on
as this was the season for outdoor location work. But on
floor no. 1, where they had been shooting a week ago, they
had left a set standing for us to see.

This turned out to be the interior of a dining room. What
really drew my attention more than the decor was a light-

weight crane set up on aluminium rails. This seemed just the kind of thing that we ought to have here, but do not.

At the back of the set was a raised platform—also obviously meant for a set—the only indication of it now being the sky backdrop. We got up and walked on the platform to see if it made the hollow noise that ours do and found that it did not. Tiny electric bulbs hung in front of the backdrop. They served as stars for nocturnal scenes, we were told.

We noticed there were lights and accessories in plenty, and a general air of cleanliness—both of which are woefully lacking in our own studios in Bengal. But I did not notice any marked superiority over the best studios in Bombay and Madras.

We were next driven round the 'lot' to give us an idea of the layout of the place, and finally arrived at a projection theatre. We were to see excerpts from recent Soviet films.

The theatre was quite large—holding 500—and got so packed that many had to keep standing. There was a distribution of leaflets followed by a speech, and an introduction of the main actors featured in the excerpts. Then, at last, the lights dimmed.

Excerpt I is not an excerpt at all, but a two-reeler comedy in colour featuring three rustic characters—a sort of Russian 3 Stooges—performing age-old slapstick turns. The originality consists in the rural setting, and in the fact that there were no words. Some clever trick-work enlivens the action, and the music is inventive. Judging from the reaction of the Russians in the audience—this is obviously a very popular genre.

Excerpt II is from a film-version of a popular Russian operetta. Colour again. Good decor, good costume, good old-fashioned operetta tunes. Hardly noteworthy otherwise.

Next comes the *pièce de résistance*: two reels of Samsonov's *Optimistic Tragedy*—a Cannes prize-winner of a year ago. Made in black and white and wide screen, it casts an immediate spell. Soldiers about to leave for the front (World War I) dance on the boat-deck with their sweethearts. A slow, sombre waltz, the shuffle of dancing feet on wooden planks, and not a word spoken for full ten minutes. What holds, primarily, are the faces, held in long close-ups with a gently swaying camera. Even the close-ups of people not dancing are shot with a camera that moves gently from side to side in rhythm with the music. An unobtrusive but bold experiment that comes off beautifully.

The sequence of the march that follows is strongly reminiscent of old Russian films in staging and composition. This is followed by some intimate scenes of dialogue where there is some more harking back to the Thirties.

This seems to be a characteristic of the new Russian films, even the best of them—*Ballad of a Soldier, Forty-first, Cranes are Flying,* and now *Optimistic Tragedy*—all have this quality of echoing, occasionally, past methods, past styles, past moods. Superficially—particularly in some of the cutting and the movements of the camera—a modern, bold, unconventional approach shows through; but in almost everything else (particularly in the psychological interplay of characters) there seems to be a lack of awareness of the extended analytical powers of the medium.

A small group of us sit in the office of the Institute preparatory to being taken round the various departments. The Director of the Institute sits behind a table answering questions. At a small table in a corner sits Lev

Kuleshov—one-time film-theorist, and now a professor of the Institute.

I put the question to the Director: Is it possible—in the five-year course that the Institute offers—to turn every student admitted into the direction class into reasonably good film makers? It is Kuleshov who answers. He says that the Institute takes a year to find out if a student admitted into the direction class has it in him to make a film maker. A certain degree of natural talent is a *sine qua non*. If he turns out to be a dud at the end of the year, he is politely asked to take up some other course.

We are finally taken out on our tour, and as we move from department to department, we find ourselves getting cumulatively impressed. The students here lack nothing for a complete film education. The library is a dream. And not just the film library : there is a general library that would do credit to any university. An art department teaches all branches of painting and graphic arts. The section for the training of art directors is cluttered with models of sets which the students have used for their class-work films. One wall of the room is plastered with sketches of what look like scenes from some epic. They turn out to be visualisations done by a student for *War and Peace* which Bondarchuk is actually using for his film.

At the end of our tour of the departments we are taken by the Director to a small projection theatre where we look at two student-films. One, a documentary on the Institute itself, shows how the various departments work and how the work is coordinated into the making of a film. We spotted Mongoloid faces—Indonesian and Vietnamese, we are told. The second film—a short story involving school children—is simplicity itself, and speaks highly of the observation and inventiveness of the maker. A most promising work. We leave the Institute thoroughly impressed.

Chukhrai being on the jury, I got to know him quite well; at least as well as one can get to know a person through an interpreter. Rapport was helped by the fact that he and I had very similar reactions to the films in competition, except where the Soviet entries were concerned. There he was guarded and evasive in his comments. 'Perhaps you don't have the same problems in India as we have here' was all he would say.

I noticed that his judgment of comedies was a little unsure. At a jury meeting Chukhrai spoke up for an Argentinian comedy which all the rest of us thought pretty poor. Chukhrai disintegrated under the onslaught and finally admitted that he was not in a position to evaluate comedies because 'we get to see so few, and make even fewer, in Russia.'

One day I asked Chukhrai why he had made only three films in the space of seven years. Did he not wish to make them more frequently? Did he not *like* making films?

'Oh yes, I do. I'm so fond of the studio that when I'm not shooting myself I go and watch my friends at work.'

'But what stops you from shooting? Why aren't you shooting now, for instance?'

'You see—there's a Committee, and we have to have the approval of the Committee on the scripts first.'

'I see.'

Chukhrai probably sensed my disappointment and hastened to add : 'But we've been trying to form an Experimental Films Division so that young directors might be free to try out fresh ideas. I've been working on this a good bit of the time these last three years . . .'

It was Chukhrai who, at my request, introduced me to Mark Donskoi.

'So you like my *Childhood of Gorki*?' he said. 'And what do you think of the Soviet films in competition?'

I wasn't prepared for this question and hemmed and hawed a little.

'You see,' I managed at last, 'I'm on the jury, so I'm not supposed to talk.'

'Oh, come, come...' Donskoi gave me a hefty slap on the back, 'you don't have to hide—not from me. I'm not so stupid as to have any illusions about them. *They are bad*. I couldn't sleep two nights after seeing *Baluyev*. Why do they make them so bad? And why show them in competition?'

1964

The Gold Rush 🖋

The astonishing thing about *The Gold Rush** is that each
time you see it—no matter how long after you saw it the
last time—it seems both endearingly familiar and inex-
haustibly fresh. And it leaves you with a feeling of wanting
to see it again. It is like some great piece of music which
you know every bar of and yet would sooner listen to again
than to something new and unfamiliar.

Part of the delight and wonder derives, of course,
from Chaplin himself. Watching him, you realise that
he must be one of the very few artists of the twentieth
century who is able to completely disarm a critic at one
moment and, at the next, challenge his sharpest faculties
and come out unscathed. If one thinks of Mozart and *The
Magic Flute* and the knockabout foolery of Papageno
merging into the sublimity of Sarastro, it is because the
comparison is a valid one. Here is the same distilled
simplicity, the same purity of style, the same impeccable
craftsmanship. And the slight tinge of disappointment
at the happy ending—the sudden veering towards a

---

*Written and directed by Charles Chaplin. Commentary written
and spoken by Charles Chaplin. Photography: Rollie Totheroh and
Jack Wilson. Cast: Charlie Chaplin, Mack Swain, Tom Murray,
Georgia Hale, Betty Morissey, Malcolm Waite, Henry Bergman, and
others.

bright key after the subtle chromaticism of all that has gone before—isn't that rather like the cheery epilogue to *Don Giovanni*?

The richness of a Chaplin film derives from an infinite number of elements that go to make up his simplest statements. Take a single scene: the eating of the shoe on Thanksgiving Day. We marvel, first of all, at its enormous effectiveness as a symbol of the state to which man can be driven by hunger. But Chaplin is not content merely to hit upon a symbol. Having done so, he must proceed to embellish it with all manner of nuances. It is as if he knows he has a gem of an idea which he must slowly and lovingly turn around to make all its facets sparkle.

The scene opens with the cooking of the shoe which the Little Fellow performs with all the finesse of a French chef. This immediately strikes a note of profound ambivalence which sets our aesthetic response on edge. A casual shot of the chef's burlap-wrapped left foot indicates the source of the 'food'.

When the shoe is served, we are thrilled to discover its undeniable resemblance to an actual meat dish—with its tender and tough 'portions', its bones (the nails), and the lace which a twist of the fork would turn into spaghetti.

Offered the bony part, Big Jim rejects it, and helps himself to the tenderer uppers. Undaunted, Chaplin turns the suave gourmet, oozes high-bred relish as he sucks each nail for marrow. Big Jim takes tentative bites, and his deepening frown provides the rounding-off comment: a shoe does not make the best of dinners at the worst of times.

What the scene primarily induces is, of course, laughter; but while we double up and hold our sides, our mind soars to a plane of high aesthetic delight.

And this is true of nearly all the scenes in the film. It is never just laughter, but laughter with a complex edge to it. Sometimes, as in the Dance of the Rolls, a note is struck—and again one thinks of Mozart—which rises above comedy or pathos and can only be described as sublime.

I know it is hard to do so, but if, watching *The Gold Rush*, you can take your mind and eyes away from Chaplin for a while and concentrate on subsidiary details, you will notice that perfection extends to every aspect of a shot, to every action of the smallest bit player. With its full weight on the visuals, silent comedy demanded precision of action to a degree unknown in the era of sound. And it was not just precision of acrobatics, but precision, also, in the use of cutting and of the camera. It was all part of a highly complex and specialised art, and in *The Gold Rush* we see it in a state of ultimate refinement.

The great silent comedians also realised the importance of believable settings for their stories; for these provided the ground-bass of sanity over which the slapstick could have its full contrapuntal play. Thus in *The Gold Rush*, the snow-bound hazards of gold prospecting are a constant and convincing *visual* presence. Even when a blizzard blows the cabin away and lands it on the edge of a precipice, the sheer technical expertise of the scene puts us in the right mood to enjoy the inspired comic business that follows.

Seeing *The Gold Rush* now, one cannot help reflecting a little sadly that Chaplin's resistance to the talkies was after all a very genuine one. *Monsieur Verdoux, Limelight, The Great Dictator*—all had moments of greatness. But even as a humanist and a social satirist, Chaplin's words have never quite matched the eloquence of his pantomime. As for his musical, Mozartian quality, it had gradually dwindled until, in *A King in New York*, one found no trace of it at all.

1964

Little Man, Big Book ✍

Now that it is out and we have read it, it is a little difficult to recall precisely what sort of a book* we had been expecting from Charles Chaplin.

Of course, it had to be a big book. With a professional life stretching over sixty years and spanning two centuries, a mere recounting of the various transitions—from music hall to legitimate theatre, from theatre to screen, and from silent movies to sound ones—would fill a volume. And Chaplin, as we all know, took time off for other pursuits as well.

Perhaps the book would give us an insight into his mind and his methods? After all, is he not the only artist in history who has been universally accepted, admired and acclaimed? And what about the contradictions that deepened and blurred contours of the man? Would there, perhaps, be some probing self-analysis which would make them coalesce into a clear and comprehensible whole?

Having read the book leaves one with an odd feeling. You know this is not quite what you expected, and yet it has given you enough insight into the man to tell you that this was the only kind of book he could have written.

The insight comes as much from what he says as from

---

*Charles Chaplin, *My Autobiography*. The Bodley Head, London, 1964.

what he withholds. One of the main faults of the second part of the book is that it does not probe enough. And yet, this very want of probing, being consistent, helps in the end in a kind of oblique revelation.

All this is not to imply that Chaplin has so far been a figure shrouded in mystery. As long as we can remember, we have known about the rags-to-riches fairy tale aspect of his life. We knew of his gift of mime which his mother so lovingly nurtured; we knew, vaguely, of a gypsy somewhere back among his ancestors. But more than anything else, we knew him as the man who could make you laugh one minute and bring a lump to your throat the next as no one else had ever done before or since. And of course we knew the Little Man, the Tramp. To us Charlie and the Tramp were one and the same person. Shorn of his costume and make-up, Charlie was someone we did not know and did not care to know.

The image of the Little Man was sharp and clear when *City Lights* came out in 1931. Sound had already come, but Charlie refused to speak. Bravo! What need of speech when one could say so much with a lift of the eyebrow and a shrug of the shoulder?

After *City Lights*, a gap of four years. Why, we complained, did he not make films oftener? It seemed unfair that there should be such long waits between them: Oughtn't he to be like a circus, turning up once every year to dole out its perennial delights?

In *Modern Times*, Charlie suffered odd reflexes, tightening nuts on conveyor belts. There were two passages of sound: the Big Boss bawling out invectives via a mammoth television screen, and Charlie singing a song in eloquent gibberish. We still rejoiced in the persistent image.

But Chaplin, we learnt, had married his leading lady. First marriage? No, the third. So it was Charlie who was gauche with girls: Chaplin seemed to have quite a way with them! The image split a tiny bit.

With *The Great Dictator*, Charlie retired into his niche for good, and Chaplin took over. This Chaplin spoke English with a British accent, satirised contemporary political tyrants and spoke in eloquent condemnation of war and man's hatred against man.

With this transition from the timeless universal to the contemporary particular, began the ruthless journalistic tirade which set out to destroy the world's favourite symbol —the underdog kicked about and yet surviving in a world of privileged morons and monsters. With growing horror and dismay, one watched the spectacle of Chaplin turned into a sort of quick-change villain—by turns a rake, a Red, an evader of income tax, a Scrooge, a plagiarist and almost any other ignominious role that a malicious and vindictive Press could invent.

And there was also the spectacle, disturbing and unfamiliar, of Chaplin anxious to defend his moral position and fight back his detractors. Perhaps, deep down in our hearts, we were naive enough to believe that he should have been able to shrug it all off with the nonchalance of the Tramp himself—and amble off towards his next masterpiece.

Such, of course, could never be. And the book very largely reveals why.

Up to the point where the Tramp image persists, the book achieves a rare combination of warmth, intimacy, and sharp observation. The combination of the tragic and the comic that characterises his films also marks the best passages of this section, and whole chunks of it, one feels, could serve as ready material for film scripts.

Blurring of factual details over the years does not seem to bother him, and we too find ourselves caring less and less about the veracity and yielding to the persuasiveness of the writing. 'After all, there are more facts and details in works of art than in history books'—says Chaplin, extolling Eisenstein's film of *Ivan*. One feels that this is the kind of facts and details he aims at and achieves in writing of his childhood. People and places, moods and incidents, come vibrantly alive:

> It poured with rain during the service, the grave-diggers threw down clods of earth on the coffin which resounded with a brutal thud. It was macabre and horrifying and I began to weep. Then the relatives threw in their wreaths and flowers. Mother, having nothing to throw in, took my precious black-bordered handkerchief. 'Here, sonny,' she whispered, 'this will do for both of us.'

One does not look for facts: one listens, rather, to the persistent ring of truth, and realises that this, with Chaplin, is as it should be.

Whatever liberties Chaplin may have taken with details, there is no doubting the rich drama and eventfulness of the early years. One feels it is not the fact of poverty alone that accounts for it; it is a combination of that and the fact that, whatever the circumstances, the Chaplins strove to preserve the aura of their glamorous professional past:

> Mother always stood outside her environment and kept an alert ear on the way we talked, correcting our grammar and making us feel that we were distinguished.

Father, long estranged from Mother, was for a long time a remote figure—viewed and worshipped from a distance. But Mother's insanity and subsequent deportation to an asylum brought Father and Son together for a brief spell. 'He fascinated me,' writes Chaplin. 'At meals I watched every move he made, the way he ate, the way he held his knife, as though it were a pen, when cutting his meat. And for years I copied him.'

All this we recognise as the source of the mimicry that Chaplin was later to apotheosise. Helped by brother Sydney —older by six years—Chaplin's professional career began early. By the time he was in his teens he had already acquired a sizeable experience and a measure of reputation. 'The word Art never entered my head. The theatre meant a livelihood and nothing more.' The youthful Mozart might have made the same sort of comment. You either have a gift of melody or you do not. If you do, it is difficult to think of writing a tune as a consciously creative process. It is the same with mime. Great clowns are great distillers of human experience; and what is art except a process of distillation? Feel as he might about it, Chaplin was already well on the way to becoming an artist.

While the first half of the book mainly concerns the transition from stage to screen—from rags to riches, shall we say—it also gives hints of the contradictions that were later to deepen and lead eventually, and perhaps inevitably, to a 'getting away from it all'.

The phenomenal climb up the financial ladder was as much due to his wide and immediate popular acceptance as to the shrewd manoeuvring (even without the aid of brother Sydney) of business deals with hard-boiled movie magnates. It was inevitable that success of this sort would have all manner of unforeseen repercussions. Consider the circumstances—a mimetic genius given the freedom to proliferate in a medium which not only meant reaching a worldwide audience, but which, by its very nature, endowed his art with an abstract, timeless quality. The hoariest of knock-about turns—custard-pie throwing—had already proved on the screen to assume the dignity of ballet.

No wonder Chaplin was able to win acclaim as an artist in such a short space of time.

Stage could have never given him this reputation. His sporadic education, his slum background, his amorous misadventures—nothing could bar his entry now into the highest intellectual circles. With actors and musicians—that is to say, with interpretative artists—Chaplin felt quite at home. The great Nijinsky, who had come to watch his shooting, actually incurred his irritation. 'On the last day I told my cameraman not to put film in the camera, knowing Nijinsky's doleful presence would ruin my attempts to be funny.'

With men of letters, however, as well as with scientists and politicians, Chaplin could only prevaricate, or be facetious, or naive. And this—as the frequent record of conversations suggests—without being fully conscious of it. He once met Hart Crane, the American poet in Greenwich village. 'We discussed the purpose of poetry. I said it was a love letter to the world. He spoke of my work being in the tradition of Greek comedies. I told him I had tried to read an English translation of Aristophanes, but couldn't finish it.'

This is only one example of the kind of thing that clutters up the entire second half of the book. Not that the portraits of celebrities lack observation; Nehru, for instance, is particularly vivid, discoursing on politics in a car going at seventy miles an hour; but they are all on a physical plane, which is the least one can expect from an artist of Chaplin's calibre. On the intellectual level, he seems to have had no access at all. The encounter with Brecht sums this up nicely. 'At Hanns Eisler's we used to meet Bertolt Brecht, who looked decidedly vigorous with his cropped head, and, as I remember, was always smoking a cigar. Months later I showed him the script of *Monsieur*

Verdoux, which he thumbed through. His only comment: "Oh, you write a script Chinese fashion." ' That's all.

The idea that Chaplin is an intuitive artist—one of the few 'primitives' of the cinema—is strengthened by his occasional dissertation on the aesthetics of film making. He says on the use of the camera: 'My own camera set up is based on facilitating choreography for the actors' movements. When a camera is placed on the floor and moves about the player's nostrils, it is the camera that is giving the performance and not the actor.' Anyone with a modicum of familiarity with the aesthetics of cinema knows that a camera cannot give a performance. It is the director who expresses himself in a particular manner through a particular use of the camera. The truth is that Chaplin, being his own director, was perhaps never truly conscious of the director as a separate entity.

The second half of the book falls quickly into a pattern, which is something like this—germination of a film idea; the making of the film, followed by post-release tension, relieved, inevitably, by public acclaim and accumulating profits; then an account of a period of non-creativity, marked either by luxurious relaxation in the company of affluent friends (Hearst is counted among the best!) or by amorous bouts with generously endowed females (on Joan Barry: 'upper regional domes immensely expansive and made alluring by an extremely low décolleté summer dress which, in the drive home, evoked my libidinous curiosity'); accounts of hobnobbing with the great; *cliché* dissertations on Art and Life; accounts of lawsuits and the growing belligerence of the U.S. Press, the Federal Court and Rightist factions, followed by accounts of countering charges and inevitable self-exculpation.

The cumulative effect of all this is to make one feel that if this was the only way to write the book it should not have been written at all. Indignation at the U.S.A.'s treatment of a great artist is already an old feeling with us. The only new thing in the book in this respect is Chaplin's persistent anxiety to clear his own name. 'Later my lawyer called up, his voice vibrant, "Charlie, you are exonerated. The blood test proves you cannot be the father." "This," I said emotionally, "is retribution!" '

Chaplin builds up the last section of the book to a crescendo of happiness and contentment. Goodness knows he deserves all this—a happy marriage, a home, children getting the best European education, and the peace of mind and the leisure to write a fat book of memoirs.

Doubtless, also, his artistic instinct dictated that there should be no jarring notes in this jubilant finale. Otherwise how to explain the total absence from this portion of his last film and his only failure: *A King in New York*? Did Chaplin feel it would too readily invoke Calvero of his own *Limelight*—the ageing clown who had lost his ability to make people laugh?

1964

Akira Kurosawa ✒

I first learnt about Kurosawa from Dilys Powell's account of the 1951 Venice Film Festival in the *Sunday Times*. *Rashomon* had just been screened: the first film from post-war Japan—and one of the very first ever—to be presented to a discerning European audience. 'Violent action alternating with passages of calm', 'virtuoso cutting and camerawork', 'masterly acting by the bandit' . . . these are some of Powell's phrases which stick in my mind. She also made it clear that the impact of the film had been both deep and wide and that it was, in fact, being tipped for the Lion.

The fact that *Rashomon* did win the Grand Prix, and was acquired by RKO for world distribution, made it possible for us to see it in Calcutta within a year of Venice. The originality of the story, its undercurrent of eroticism, the obvious virtuoso aspects of its technique, and the fact that it was the first Japanese film ever to be shown here, made it a popular film with the Bengali audience. *Rashomon* is the only serious artistic foreign film to have been frequently revived at Sunday morning shows.

The effect of the film on me, personally, was electric. I saw it three times on consecutive days and wondered each time if there was another film anywhere which gave such sustained and dazzling proof of a director's command over every aspect of film making. Even after fifteen years,

whole chunks of the film come vividly back to mind in all
their visual and aural richness: the woodcutter's journey
through the forest, shot with a relentless tracking camera
from an incredible variety of angles—high, low, back and
front—and cut with axe-edge precision; the bandit's first
sight of the woman as she rides by, her veil lifted momenta-
rily by a breeze, while he lolls in the shade of a tree, slap-
ping away at mosquitoes; the striking formality of the court
scene with the judge never seen at all; the scene of witch-
craft with the medium whirling in a trance, and the wind
blowing from two opposite directions at the same time . . .
No, there was no doubt the Japanese cinema was something
to reckon with, and a good probe into its past achievements
was called for.

The probe did happen, and in a surprisingly short time
we began to hear of directors like Ozu, Mizoguchi, Kinu-
gasa, Gosho, and Ichikawa—all with long lists of past
achievements to their credit, and all virtually unknown outside the tiny island of Japan. Since then, all the standard
histories of the cinema have had substantial chapters on
the school of Japan incorporated in their new editions. The
Cinémathèque in Paris and the NFT in London have had
seasons of Japanese masters. Every festival in every country
now has at least one Japanese film in competition every
year. Young directors like Teshigahara and Hani have
emerged and made their mark. But it is still the maker of
Rashomon—Akira Kurosawa—who maintains the strongest
foothold abroad; and it is to a study of this director that
Donald Richie devotes what must be one of the most lavish
film books* ever.

What fits Richie particularly well for the task is that he
has not only lived in Japan for a long time and knows

---

*Donald Richie, *The Films of Akira Kurosawa*. University of California Press, 1965.

its language and culture, but he has a cultured response to the cinema as an art. He has also been close to Kurosawa long enough to have got an insight into the man as well as his methods of work. All this makes him responsive to the broader aspects of Kurosawa's work—which include western influences—as well as to its native nuances. He is thus able to make definitive statements about sources of style instead of the usual vague or sweeping attributions to Noh and Kabuki.

The plan of the book is admirable. There is a biographical introduction with copious quotes from Kurosawa, as well as from some of his closest associates. This is followed by a study of individual films in chronological order. Each film is given a separate chapter, which in turn is subdivided into sections on Story, Casting, Production, etc. Then comes a long general study of Kurosawa's technique taken stage by stage from scripting to music. At the end, there is an exhaustive filmography.

Among the various elements in Kurosawa's work, there are two that generate some mystification. One is the stress on action, even on violence: the Kurosawa combats are among the most violent ever filmed. Is this a Japanese trait? If so, why is it absent from the work of th, two other great Japanese masters—Ozu and Mizoguchi?

The other element is the somewhat musty didacticism most noticeable in his contemporary stories. This too seems a trait peculiar to Kurosawa, as no other Japanese master shows it in quite the same degree.

Although Richie does not precisely relate these traits to any sources, there are enough clues in the book—most of all in the quotes from Kurosawa himself—which enable us to piece them together and draw our own conclusions. 'I am the kind of person,' says Kurosawa, 'that works violently, throwing myself into it. I also like hot summers, cold winters, heavy rains and snows, and I think most of my pictures have that. I like extremes because I find them most alive . . .'

This seems to me the direct opposite of Ozu and Mizoguchi. But this does not necessarily make Kurosawa less Japanese. As even a cursory study of their history shows, the Japanese are by no means a simple people lending themselves to easy categorisation. Contradictory traits abound. The national character reveals markedly militarist tendencies throughout history, although the arts have all along maintained a serenity achieved through a rigid formalism.

Kurosawa himself is of Samurai stock. His father was one of the last of the military educators. The very first film of Kurosawa, *Sanshiro Sugata*, had as its basis the conflict between judo and ju-jit-su. Action, therefore, may be said to have been a main preoccupation with Kurosawa from the very beginning.

But even before he started making films, Kurosawa had been an avid film-goer. The few directors he names as his favourites are all American: Ford, Wyler, Capra, Stevens, Hawks. I do not think it would be too far-fetched to assume that Ford was Kurosawa's mentor for the scenes of mass battle as well as of individual combat. The feeling of heartiness that pervades Kurosawa's Samurai film, as well as the horseplay and the repeated use of the same players in typed parts, are all there in Ford's Westerns too.

The didactic tone may well have come from the Capra of *Deeds* and *Smith* and *John Doe*. There is the same tendency to pounce on a social evil and expose it through the agency of an idealist protagonist. The difference is that while Capra peppers his didacticism with his peculiar American brand of whimsy, Kurosawa lets in nothing lighter than irony.

Compounded with these influences is that of the great
nineteenth century Russian novelists: Tolstoy, Dostoevsky,
Turgenev ('I go back to them again and again'). It is to
these that Kurosawa owes the probing quality of his scripts.
This is a novelistic trait which at its best produces a *Seven
Samurai*, or an *Ikiru*. Even at its worst—parts of *The Bad
Sleep Well* and *High and Low*—it still invests the film with a
basic seriousness which is a rare virtue in a film maker at all
times. The failure is mainly on the thematic level, or in the
mechanics of plot-making, or in the emphasis on certain
elements which are passé from a sophisticated western
viewpoint.

In *Ikiru*, which is surely the finest of his contemporary
essays, these defects are not there, as the plot grows from
the characters. But *Ikiru* has an aspect to it which needs
to be examined.

In the second half of the film, Kurosawa's ruthless de-
piction of character and motivation reaches its height.
But the preoccupation with it is so great that at times
the film runs close to losing all plasticity, and thereby all
visual interest. Richie says of *Seven Samurai* that 'here Kurosawa insisted, more than in any other single film, that
motion picture be composed entirely of motion'. Judged
against this dictum, the almost total staticity of the second
half of *Ikiru* appears all the more strange.

And yet, in his adaptation of *Macbeth*, Kurosawa for-
sakes verbal poetry for the poetry of action. One suspects
he could do this because, not knowing English, he was able
to escape the spell of Shakespeare's poetry which has either
inhibited all film versions of Shakespeare in English, or
else brought forth bastard versions which make vain attempts to be faithful both to the bard and to the demands
of the film medium.

Even the lesser works of Kurosawa show a grasp of technique which is truly astonishing. He is, first of all, a master of cutting. 'For me,' says Kurosawa, 'shooting only means getting something to edit.' While we need not take this as literally true, Kurosawa's very method of shooting suggests his deep concern about continuity (the 'flowing quality', as Kurosawa says) in both its physical and its emotional aspects. He shoots his films in sequence—an expensive procedure which few directors can afford. He also shoots with multiple cameras—another expensive method—which automatically solves some of the more taxing continuity problems. His sound track—always composed with meticulous care—also adds to the feeling of fluency.

But it is this very quality which keeps him within the bounds of tradition and cuts him off from all the trends that mark the newly emerging western *avant-garde*. Here is another quote from Kurosawa that is significant in this context: 'It is just because a director has something to say that he finds the form, the skill, the technique to bring it out. If you are concerned only with *how* you say something, without having anything to say, then even the way you say something won't come to anything . . . Techniques do not enlarge a director. They limit him. Technique alone, with nothing to support its weight, always crushes the basic idea which should prevail.'

One can easily oppose this statement by saying that a director has always something to say, no matter how trivial or portentous, and more often than not, when a director has nothing of much importance to say, he will rely more on technique. Hitchcock, of course, is the classic example of this. In Hitchcock at his best, the basic idea is not crushed, but transcended by the technique which becomes something to be admired for its own sake. This has happened in the cinema again and again, in Westerns, in thrillers, in slapstick comedies, in musicals. And the same thing has happened in Kurosawa's lesser efforts where we come across passages where the director has triumphed over the scenarist.

But there is no mention in Richie's book of Hitchcock, nor of Godard, Truffaut or Resnais, nor of anybody of the 1960s for that matter. Antonioni is mentioned once as a director whom Kurosawa 'admires', but 'is not influenced by'. I feel this is a regrettable omission in a book published in 1965 about a director who is one of the leading figures in contemporary cinema. One is forced to conclude that Kurosawa does not greatly care about the new paths that are being explored.

But perhaps this is not so surprising after all. There is nothing in the Japanese artistic tradition to support the slapdash methods of a Godard; and Kurosawa, in spite of his western influences, may well be more of a Japanese at heart than we think.

1966

Tokyo, Kyoto and Kurosawa ✍

We were on our way back to Tokyo from Kyoto. The time
was around midday. Pink-cheeked girls in uniforms wheeled
food-trolleys up and down the gangway of the compartment, selling packaged curry and rice. A loudspeaker
offered the use of a telephone with connections to Osaka,
Kyoto, Yokohama and Tokyo. Sitting by the large window
and watching the landscape whiz past, one felt at the
point of being airborne. And no wonder. This new electric
train on the Hokkaido line had an average speed of 125
miles an hour—and I noticed no *ritardando* for bridges and
tunnels.

On the onward journey, we had been lucky to get a clear
view of Fuji, its peak brushed pink by the low sun flatten-
ing perceptibly as it dipped towards the horizon. But this
time, on the way back, Fuji was more characteristically
shrouded in mist and chimney-smoke.

My all too brief Japanese visit was drawing to its end,
and Fuji was one of a hundred impressions which formed
a whirling *collage* in my mind. Tokyo itself—audaciously
modern, aspiring, ebullient. I like big cities to engulf and
bewilder me, and Tokyo does this with a persistence un-
approached by other big cities. For a measure of the city's
assault on the senses, one has only to take a walk down
the Ginza of an evening, with one eye on the road for the
traffic, and the other up on the animated neons which,

for variety, invention, and rhythmic complexity, have no parallel.

Strange to reflect that the same Japanese mind produced the Zen gardens—surely the most subtle and self-effacing of artistic pursuits. One unresponsive to the feel and texture of rocks, foliage and water, or one who thinks of gardens in terms of the predictable symmetries of a Mogul Bagh will in all likelihood miss the gentle harmony of contrasts that permeates these gardens. The work of the artist—the order imposed on natural elements—is so muted as to be barely discernible. And yet that is what makes works of art of these gardens.

The temple of the Thousand Buddhas, in Kyoto, had the life-size idols ranged in galleries like crowd in a football stadium. The dull gold of the statues gleaming in the dim light of the cavernous hall, and the sheer weight of numbers, produced the right awe-inspiring effect. But one could not help feeling that the main preoccupation here was religious, not aesthetic. Art consisted, as in most Japanese temples, in the beauty of the woodwork, the tiles, and the proportions of the architecture.

Deer roamed the famous park at Nara. As you walked up the driveway towards the temple, they came prancing up and nudged you with the soft tips of their lopped-off antlers, expecting biscuits which you could buy by the dozen from shops which lined the path. Inside the temple, the colossal Buddha sat obscured by incense-smoke between gigantic metal lotuses of an unbelievable art-nouveauish ugliness.

And yet how wonderful it was to roam the streets of old Kyoto and just look at the old houses. Doors, windows, rooftops, gates, cornices were all works of art, and the balancing of beauty and function a consistent miracle.

The human element in Japan was dominated, in my mind, by school children. Wherever we went sightseeing, there they were, in great uniformed hordes, tumbling merrily out of sleek school buses, or gathered in earnest knots with necks craned to converge on teacher scattering educative data.

On our way to Nara, a brief diversion had taken us through the woods where *Rashomon* was filmed. These were up in the mountains, and one could just as well have been on the Kalimpong Road. As I sat in the train, I thought of the woods, of the strange and powerful film shot there, and of my imminent encounter with the maker of that film: at the end of my journey lay a lunch appointment with Akira Kurosawa.

I only hoped it would not be in a Japanese inn, as most other meals so far had been. The interiors of these inns —especially the old, hallowed ones—afford great aesthetic delight. I never tired of running my eyes over the lines of the *tatame*, so spotlessly clean that the thought of cockroaches barely formed in the mind before it perished. But—and this was my only serious quarrel with Japan—I could accept neither the food they served, nor the fact that you had to genuflect in order to eat it. Moreover, I do not think the best food in the world can be truly relished unless transferred from plate to mouth with ease and in the right quantity. Chopsticks in the hands of a beginner are apt to thwart these basic functions.

As it turned out, the venue for the meeting was a Chinese restaurant in a quiet back street of Tokyo. 'A favourite of Kurosawa's,' said Mrs Kawakita, my hostess and a close friend of the director. At least one could face the gastronomic hazards with more confidence here.

Kurosawa turned out to be that rarity—a tall Japanese. He also had a stoop, with an appropriate humility to go with it, kindly eyes which a ready smile thinned into more slits, and a hushed and gentle tone of voice—all of which was in unexpected contrast to the ferocious image derived from his samurai films. But then, it is not unusual to find schizophrenics among people of the theatrical profession, and I knew Kurosawa had samurai blood in him. I had visions of his unbridled other self, pitching into that scene of combat with all the controlled fury of a samurai himself.

I started by talking of *Seven Samurai*, which turned out to be both his and my favourite amongst his films. 'It needs long and hard training to be a film samurai,' he said. 'There was so much about the samurai that was stylised—his ride, his run, the way he wielded the sword. A samurai would never be hunched over his saddle when charging. He would stand straight up with feet firmly on the stirrups and knees pressed tight against the flanks of the horse. His body would not be perpendicular, but leaning forward at an angle to prevent being thrown backwards by the force of the charge.'

Kurosawa rose from his chair to demonstrate the stance of the charging samurai.

'And about the sword—it wouldn't cut at all if you only hacked with it. You would have to combine' (more demonstration here) 'a *backing* motion with a *slicing* motion. And when the samurai runs, his head shouldn't bob up and down with his footsteps. The effect should be like a swift floating. In other words, the head shouldn't trace a wavy curve, but a straight line.'

A stickler for historical accuracy, Kurosawa, in his period films, makes his actors put on period costumes obtained from museums.

'But you know where the snag is,' he said with a twinkle in his eyes. 'The Japanese as a whole have grown smaller over the last five or six hundred years. It is difficult to find actors large enough for these costumes to fit.'

I asked if he had any more samurai films in mind.

'None,' he said. 'And I doubt if I could ever make another one.'

'Why not?'

'Because there's such a dearth of horses now. You see, most of the horses used in films came from farms. But now farm-work has been mechanised, and horses are bred only for racing.'

The conversation now turned to Kurosawa's *Macbeth*, which had a most impressive array of horses in it. But I was more interested in the birds—the birds from Birnam wood which invade Macbeth's castle after the trees of the wood have been cut down. I said I thought the idea a brilliant one.

'Well, the trees obviously had birds nesting in them, and the birds obviously had to go somewhere, so I made them invade the castle. But,' and here his eyes twinkled again, 'we had trouble filming them. The idea was to have them wildly flapping about above the heads of the actors. But they were not trained birds, and they just kept flopping down on the floor as we released them and stayed there. Some even kept slipping, because we had polished the floor with wax. It took us a whole week to do that one scene properly.'

It appeared that Laurence Olivier had liked Kurosawa's idea of showing Lady Macbeth as pregnant—because it gave a clear motivation to her actions—and had written to ask if he might borrow it for his production of the play. In course of the letter Olivier had remarked, somewhat gratuitously, that he believed the child born of the Macbeths would be an ugly and deformed one. To Kurosawa this had seemed like a crude and inartistic comment, and he had consequently turned down Olivier's request.

I had heard that Kurosawa had been signed up by the American producer Joe Levine to direct a film in the USA. The news had intrigued me, because this would be the first instance of an Asian director with only a rudimentary knowledge of English making an English-language film in the States.

Mrs Kawakita had hinted earlier that Kurosawa had got into the bad books of the Japanese producers through his lordly unconcern with the financial aspects of a film. His last film, *Red Beard*, planned to be shot in six months, took more than two years to complete. This had resulted in the termination of a twenty-year-old relationship with the actor Toshiro Mifune, who had been in every Kurosawa film except one since 1947. For *Red Beard*, Mifune had signed an exclusive contract for six months and had grown a beard for the part. As the shooting dragged on, Mifune had to keep turning down offer after offer. While the film was in production, he did nothing to jeopardise its interests. But from the moment the shooting ended he has been a stranger to Kurosawa, with no chance of a rapprochement in sight.

The fact that *Red Beard* went way over budget was something Kurosawa could not care less about. All that mattered to him was perfection, which he had achieved in the film. The critics applauded *Red Beard*. It also had a long run, but not long enough to bring back the cost. Kurosawa sensed trouble and cast about for backing from abroad.

'I had a story in mind,' said Kurosawa. 'I had saved up a clipping from an American newspaper which des-

cribed how a goods train went tearing through Chicago
at eighty miles an hour with three men on board but no
one at the control. For some unaccountable reason, the
driver had jumped off and killed himself. The train as
well as the passengers were ultimately saved, and the
film will show how.'

But there were snags. Kurosawa had stipulated that
he would work with his own Japanese crew consisting of
some twenty technicians. Producer Levine's drastic terms
permitted only one English-speaking assistant. The fact
that Kurosawa had to concede could be indicative of
either his great urge to film the story at any cost, or of
the alarming situation of the serious film maker in Japan.
What is true of Kurosawa is also true of Ichikawa,
Kobayashi and Shindo.

However, a truly gifted film maker—as has often been
proved in the history of the cinema—can rise above his
circumstances; so that, Levine notwithstanding, one can
look forward to *The Runaway Train*—if it ever gets made
—with all the pleasurable anticipation of an authentic
Japanese Kurosawa. Let us hope that a charging train will
prove just as inspiring as a charging samurai.

1967

New Wave and Old Master 🖋

François Truffaut's devotion to Hitchcock has been one of the more celebrated if somewhat inscrutable facts of recent film history. This devotion came to light in the early fifties when Truffaut was on the critical staff of the distinguished French *avant-garde* film journal *Cahiers du Cinéma*. To most of the *Cahiers* clan of critics, Hitchcock was one of the Mighty Ones—on a par with Griffith and Eisenstein and Murnau—a true innovator, a stylist par excellence, a purveyor of what they termed Pure Cinema.

When Hitchcock first came to know of this adulation, he is said to have shrugged it off as typical French perversity. In his early interviews with some of the *Cahiers* critics, he invariably adopted a tone that oscillated between mock solemnity and tongue-in-cheek facetiousness. The fact is, Hitchcock was not prepared to accept a position in the hierarchy of film makers which he believed did not belong to him. As he had himself said on many occasions, he thought of himself primarily as an entertainer, peddling a unique brand of suspense spiced with horror and leavened with humour. If one looked for a literary equivalent one would find it, roughly, in a cross between Sapper, Sax Rohmer and Cornell Woolrich. Irresistible though such a hybrid might be, who would ever think of mentioning him in the same breath as, say, Shakespeare?

When, some four or five years ago, it was announced that Truffaut was going to do a book on Hitchcock, the young French critic had already undergone a change of vocation: he had turned to making films instead of writing about them. As one of the leaders of the movement which came to be known as the New Wave, Truffaut had already made two or three films which had brought him consider-able acclaim. While these films had an undeniable free-wheeling quality about them, they still belonged unmistakably to a French tradition. If they reminded one of any other director, it was Jean Renoir, and not Alfred Hitchcock. One wondered, therefore, if the book would reveal a change of attitude in Truffaut as a result of his initiation into film making. One was also curious to find out how Hitchcock would react to the probings of a professional colleague who, although he had professed great admiration for him as a critic, had clearly spurned his methods as a director.

Well, the book is here—a handsome volume with price to match—and I must say that even if the answers are not all there in so many words, there is enough between the lines to help one draw one's conclusions.

*Hitchcock** consists of a fifty-hour long tape-recorded interview conducted by Truffaut in 1962 over a month or so in the former's Hollywood home. The book is copiously and ideally illustrated with stills that cover the full forty-five-year span of Hitchcock's active professional career. Some of the more celebrated instances of 'cutting for suspense' are illustrated by a succession of stills arranged to correspond to the editing pattern in the film. Interspersed throughout the book are pictures of the Master himself, in various stages of obesity, a perpetual

---

*François Truffaut, *Hitchcock*. New York, 1967.

contradiction to the nimbleness and knife-edge precision of his best work.

The scheme that Truffaut adopts for the interview enables him to proceed chronologically, taking each film individually, and extracting as much information about it as the Master would provide. We get to know the circumstances in which a particular film was made, Hitchcock's own special reasons for making it, and the way he set about putting the screenplay on the screen. As an interviewer, Truffaut uses admirable discretion throughout. The intimate knowledge of the Master's works he reveals and the frequency with which he injects adulatory comments ensure not only wholehearted cooperation from his subject, but also a fund of anecdotes which upholds his image of a witty raconteur.

It is difficult to guess how a non-addict would react to a book like this, but to those who love the cinema, and especially to those who know and love Hitchcock for what he is—as I do—the book will prove most rewarding.

What the book fails to achieve, and in failing defeats Truffaut's main purpose in writing it, is to raise Hitchcock to the eminence of a profound and serious artist. 'If, as in the case of Ingmar Bergman,' says Truffaut in his preface, 'one accepts the premise that cinema is an art form on a par with literature, I suggest that Hitchcock belongs . . . among such artists of anxiety as Kafka, Dostoevsky and Poe.' Well, there is nothing in the interview to substantiate this claim.

The fact is, the genre that Hitchcock chose for himself debars by its very nature the kind of seriousness one associates with the writers Truffaut mentions. It is possible for a Chaplin or a Keaton, working in the genre of satirical slapstick, to plumb the depths of the human condition and rise to the level of serious artists. Even a John Ford, making a Western, can achieve the true simplicity and poetic grandeur of folk ballad. But Hitchcock is obliged to deal with characters who are supposed to exist on a level of everyday reality, and yet have no existence beyond the needs of a melodramatic plot designed solely to generate maximum suspense. Admittedly, the creation of such suspense calls for ingenuity of a very special kind; but such ingenuity can never be a concomitant of serious art. After all, it can hardly be said that Kafka, Poe and Dostoevsky are out to dazzle us with their cleverness.

The following remark by Hitchcock comes towards the end of the interview and can only be attributed to a momentary aberration caused by sustained adulation:

> 'That's what I'd like you to do—a picture that would gross millions of dollars throughout the world. It's an area of film in which it is more important for you to be pleased with technique than with the content. It's the kind of picture in which the camera takes over. Of course, some critics are more concerned with the scenario, it won't necessarily get you the best notices. But you would have to design your films just as Shakespeare does his plays—for an audience.'

It is sad that Hitchcock should be thinking here only of the ends and not the means. Surely, Shakespeare had other and more weighty preoccupations than just keeping an audience glued to their seats.

Sanity is restored when a little later Hitchcock says: 'The phase I'm trying to go through at the time is to try to correct a major weakness in my work in respect of the thin characterisations within the suspense stories. It is not so simple, because when you work with strong characters, they seem to take you where they want to go.' The note of regret here is unmistakable. It is significant that Truffaut has no comment to make on this, because this is the statement which most effectively nullifies his own thesis about the Master.

It remains to be said that in his best works (Truffaut's own favourite happily coincides with mine) such as *Rear Window*, Hitchcock manages to achieve the mysterious, unanalysable quality of true works of art. To use a favourite phase of the *Cahiers* critics, Hitchcock here achieves Pure Cinema. This refers to the unique ambience created by an inspired use of all the resources of the film maker—camera, sound, editing, mixing and so on. In Hitchcock's case, this is the result of forty-five years of sustained imaginative effort brought to bear on a single pursuit: the creation of suspense. No wonder he has mastered its mechanics to a degree which no one else ever has or ever will.

One suspects—and this is what surprises one most—that Truffaut too has an insight into the real Hitchcock when he says: 'Your point of departure is not the content but the container.' Great art, as has been proved over a very long period of time, always seeks a harmonious balance between the content and the container.

At least, this is what François Truffaut sought, and found, in that remarkable first film of his—*Les Quatre Cents Coup*.

1969

Silent Films 🖎

We know that extraordinary things have been happening
in the cinema in the last ten or fifteen years. We know
of the emergence of new schools and new styles in film
making, of the new permissiveness that marks the content of films of the West as well as the Far East. We
know of the New Wave and the legacy of unshackled
film making it has left behind. We know of the American Underground, and we also know of the collapse of
the tried and true Hollywood system of big film production, perhaps the most striking and significant event
of all.

But in addition to all this one must note another recent
phenomenon. This has nothing to do with film making,
but with film appreciation. This is the sudden upsurge
of interest in the beginnings of the cinema brought about
by a steady stream of revivals of silent films in the archives
and cinémathèques of the world. A great deal of fresh
thinking on the art of the cinema has resulted from this.
What was once patronisingly thought of as rudimentary
and backward has now emerged as valid achievements
in an independent and self-sufficient art form; an art
form with its own special appeal and its own special
aesthetics.

Today one can actually question whether the introduction of words into films was not in fact an introduction

of an impurity undermining the direct visual impact of the medium. There is no denying the fact that with the coming of sound, images in films became, in general, less meaningful in themselves. After all, with sound and with words one can always fall back on speech to convey one's meaning. When Chaplin eats his shoes in *The Gold Rush*, he performs an act which is not only funny but is also rich with overtones of symbolical meaning conveyed by purely visual means. A scene like this could never have been conceived in literary terms. And yet when Chaplin himself, in a literary mood, indulges in metaphysical pronouncements in films like *Verdoux* and *Limelight*, he conveys less sense in a less purely artistic manner than that single bit of business with the shoe in *The Gold Rush*.

It is not as if sound films do not contain moments of purely visual significance. But whenever they do they inevitably hark back to the silent cinema. And more often than not they prove to be the moments that stay in the mind longest.

There is a healthy tendency these days to try and restore the purity of the medium lost in the deluge of words, or, in other words, to find one's way back to the original sources of inspiration.

This sort of thing has happened at various times in the other arts too. Many composers have re-charged their batteries by going to the sources of folk music. Picasso sought and found inspiration in Negro sculpture. Likewise, for any modern film maker to study the works of so-called American primitives is bound to prove stimulating.

The achievements of the sound cinema are, of course, considerable. It is possible for a director who is conscious of the silent heritage to strike a satisfactory balance be-

tween sound and image. Words, too, have a valid function to perform. When written by a gifted screen writer
and spoken by an able actor, words can achieve a plastic
quality which gives them a significance that is more
cinematic than literary. But when an image or an action
speaks for itself, it acquires a level of significance in its
context which no spoken words can reach. The best of
Westerns made in Hollywood, some superior thrillers, some
comedies, some of the bucolic idylls of the French realist
schools, the best of the Japanese and the early Russian
films, and the best of the modern European works have
moments in them which hold one spellbound because they
themselves rise above the level of mere verbiage and speak
through their images.

Even the trend set by Godard, in recent times, for instance, is a predominantly visual one. The words here are
often banal and just as often improvised. This is Godard's
way of emphasising his images, which often acquire a peculiar density through being charged with all manner of
contemporary overtones.

A great many of the sound films made in the heyday
of talkies now seem dated, not just because of the weight
of words but because of the texture of their visual style.
In the period I have in mind, the star system was at its
height. This meant a cautious approach on the part of
everybody concerned in the making of a film, because
what was at stake above all was the image of the star. A
phrase used to be current in Hollywood in those days:
'go for the money.' If the cameraman had problems in
lighting a set involving a large number of actors in movement, he would be told to 'go for the money'. So was the
focus-puller who wanted to know where to keep his focus:
'go for the money.' In other words, concentrate on the
star, keep your lights on the star, keep your focus on

14

the star and to hell with the rest. This gave rise to the glamorous school of film craftsmanship. What it did, basically, was to encourage the softening of contours; and not only the contours of the star's face, but of the face of the story as well. Take the safe path, take no risks, people do not want to see hard lines in the faces of their idols, and a story with hard lines does not make for good box-office.

This is a state of affairs that did not exist in the silent era. The true stars then were the makers of the films themselves—the directors. Of course, it was not uncommon for leading actors to take to directing their own films. Many of the great slapstick comedians used to do it. But these star-directors never lost sight of the importance of the ensemble. One has only to look at a Chaplin short to see how perfectly the small parts are cast and played.

It is a fact that film makers of the silent days worked much harder and much longer on their films than their modern counterparts. There were several reasons for this. First, the apparatus. Compared with modern ones, the old tools were cumbersome. But this does not mean that they were inefficient or imperfect. It is a demonstrable fact that the ancient hand-cranked cameras produced sharper images than the modern portable Arriflexes and Camioflexes. This is because being at least four times heavier, they were at least four times less prone to vibration than the modern ones.

The second reason was that the film makers had to grapple with a language that was in the process of being evolved by the makers themselves. This meant that there were far fewer clichés to fall back upon. The director was thus forced to be creative and inventive. And observant too, because since the cinema has to do with reality as it is perceived through the eyes, the director had to re-discover meanings contained in gestures and in the concrete details of his surroundings.

It is a mistake to assume that acting in the silent cinema was exaggerated so that all one saw was flinging of arms and rolling of eyeballs. The best actors of the silent days used the minimum expressive gestures. Deprived of words, they had naturally to fall back on stylisation, but not necessarily of a sort that jarred one's sensibilities. It could afford to be subtle—except when the director deliberately aimed at larger than life effects. Mack Swain—the mountainous villain in Chaplin's films—did roll his eyes, but this was perfectly right in the context of Chaplin's approach.

Yet another reason why the film makers took longer on their films is they were not under pressures of the sort that plagued later film makers—no matter how gifted. Pressures of time, pressures of commerce, pressures from the front office. Film making in the early days was much more of a personal, intimate affair, where the artists worked lovingly and with painstaking care. Often they worked just for the love of it, with humility and with no hope of rewards, or of the kind of adulation that is showered upon some of the luminaries of the present day. In consequence of this, sadly enough, many of these artists along with their works passed quickly into oblivion.

No one has done more to try and rescue them than Kevin Brownlow. In addition to being a film maker, Brownlow was a collector of silent movies. And the more he collected, the more his conviction grew that there were many directors, many actors and many technicians of the silent period who had not been given due recognition by film historians. So Brownlow set about hunting down these figures from the past, in the United States

as well as in other parts of the world, and talking to them
and getting them to talk about their work.

The result is one of the most important film-books of
our time: *The Parade's Gone By. . . .** This is a book which
forces a revision of the conventional attitude to silent
cinema. Apart from the text which is crammed with
fascinating revelations, the hundreds of stills in the book
have incredible things to tell us about the quality of camerawork in those days, about the wonderful feeling for light
and landscape that these cameramen had, and about the
meticulous work of the set designers. Some of the big spectacles of that period—such as the Fairbanks films or *Ben
Hur* or *The Hunchback of Notre Dame*—are far superior,
visually, to their present-day Panavision technicolor counterparts, simply because better taste and better research had
gone into their designing. In fact, the key figures of the
silent period were all perfectionists. Today the trend is towards a shorthand method of film making. One goes for
the glancing, elliptical style. In this way, more often than
not, one loses in density what one gains in brevity. When
the ideas are strong the film still makes an impact. But it is
still a shorthand and therefore must lack the calligraphic
grace and beauty of the old masters. Griffith, of course,
emerges from Kevin Brownlow's book as the giant that
we knew he was. Ambitious, imaginative and immensely
hardworking, Griffith was so confident of the validity and
self-sufficiency of his art form that he made the rash
prediction that sound on film was not only scientifically
impossible but aesthetically unnecessary.

We know that Griffith was responsible for most of the
innovations in film language, but it is necessary to empha-

---

*Kevin Brownlow, *The Parade's Gone By. . . .* Secker & Warburg,
London, 1968.

sise the fact—and the book does this with great clarity—
that all his innovations came about in order to fulfil certain
expressive needs.

The most spectacular of his innovations was the crane-
shot, or rather, the precursor of the crane-shot. This occurs
in *Intolerance* in the Babylonian sequence. Here Griffith
wanted to show a Babylonian orgy and at the same time
to show that the orgy was being dwarfed by the colossal
Babylonian architecture. The problem was how to show
in the same shot the details of the people involved in the
orgy, as well as the immensity of the buildings around.
The solution was provided by Allan Dwan, himself a major
director noted for his mechanical ingenuity. Joseph Hena-
berry, who was a member of Griffith's crew at that time,
describes the taking of the shot in Kevin Brownlow's book.
He says: 'We had one of the grand shots of all times
in *Intolerance*. We built a tower facing the Babylonian set
with an elevator in it, a studio-constructed elevator. The
camera platform was mounted on top of this device. As
it descended vertically the tower moved forward on wheeled
trucks, which rode on railroad tracks. These trucks had cast
iron wheels 18″ across . . . Four people rode on the camera
platform—Griffith, Bitzer, who was Griffith's cameraman,
Karl Brown, his assistant and myself . . . Without any cut
or break it gradually descended to a medium shot which
included just the principals . . . Altogether we spent a little
more than a couple of hours on the scene. We had to
shoot with the light. If we wanted the full effect of the
settings, we had to take the scene when the lighting was
appropriate . . . So we were limited to a period between
10 a.m. and 11 a.m.'

Those who have seen *Intolerance* will know the breath-
taking effect of the shot. This is something which could
only have been conceived by someone who had something

new and important to say and was stubborn and inventive enough to devise a way of saying it.

Sound admittedly brought the cinema closer to actuality. I use the word actuality in order to suggest the surface, rather than the substance, of reality. The substance is not necessarily ensured by the addition of sound or, for that matter, of colour. I have seen many modern documentaries on poverty and other social ills which seemed less real than, say, *The Kid* or *City Lights*. And no documentary on locomotives or steamships can tell us more about them than Buster Keaton's *The General* and *The Navigator*.

The silent cinema was indeed a unique and self-sufficient art form which was wiped out of existence by commercial pressures with the coming of sound. It is a vanished art not because the artists ceased to be, but because forces stronger than theirs willed and planned its extinction. The least we can do as lovers of the cinema is to pay homage, however belated, to as many of these artists as we can and make amends for the near-sighted historian's neglect of them.

One important detail before I close. The silent film was never meant to be viewed in silence, but with the accompaniment of music. The music was usually played on the piano, sometimes on an organ and on rare occasions by an orchestra. We remember from our childhood the mellifluous tone of the Wurlitzer organ in the Palace of Varieties, which is now the Elite cinema. We also remember the tinkly pianos in the Globe, the Elphinstone, the Picture Palace. Griffith actually provided cue-sheets to theatres for music to be played by symphony orchestras along with his more ambitious films. The music had to be there not only to drown out the sound of the projector, which is why it came about in the first place, but also to provide discreet emotional embellishment to the visuals.

To improvise such accompaniment needed musicians of
a very special calibre. Today such musicians are hard to
come by anywhere in the world. So here in Calcutta, at
this session of silent revivals, let us put up cheerfully with
the noise of the projector, and be thankful for the absence
of someone who might, unwittingly, have done more harm
to the films than good.

1970

A Tribute to John Ford ✒

John Ford was nearly eighty when he died. He had
been in the film business for sixty years. By the end of
the silent era, he had already made something like fifty
films, short and long. By the time he died, he had made
well over a hundred. The most prolific of directors, Ford
was also the one who scaled the heights most frequently.
He was also remarkable in that his hallmark had remained
virtually unchanged over the last forty years, which is as
long as I have known him. A hallmark is never easy to
describe, but the nearest description of Ford's would be
a combination of strength and simplicity. The nearest
equivalent I can think of is a musical one: middle-period
Beethoven. The same boldness of contour, the simplicity
and memorability of line, the sense of architecture, even
the same outbursts of boisterousness, and the same heroic,
action-packed finales. All of this is undoubtedly best expressed in the Westerns, but is also to be met with in
some celebrated departures such as *Young Mr. Lincoln, The
Grapes of Wrath, They were Expendable, The Quiet Man.* There
were other departures, too, which lacked many of these
qualities. Near-expressionist essays, almost wholly preoccupied with the visual aspect: *The Informer, The Fugitive, The
Long Voyage Home.* And commercial chores which appeared
with despairing frequency—*Hurricane, Wee Willie Winkie,
Four Men and A Prayer*—embarrassing in their lapses of taste

and their indifferent technique. Why did such a great talent stoop to such trivialities? Ford himself gave the answer in an early interview. He said filming for him was a job which he enjoyed for its own sake. If a good story did not come his way, rather than sit about and wait for one, he would plunge into a run-of-the-mill concoction just to keep on the job.

This could mean one of two things: either Ford did not think of himself as an artist and did not care for his reputation; or he was so confident of his crests that he knew the troughs would not amount to a serious dent in his reputation in the long run. I personally believe the second to be true, simply because in no other director's work is the confidence in one's mastery so evident as in the best of John Ford. And much of his best work is undoubtedly in the Western. Like Picasso's obsession with the bull, Cézanne's with the apple, Bach's with the fugue, and the Hindu miniaturists' with the theme of Krishna, John Ford had a lifelong affair with the Western. 'When in doubt, make a Western' is reported to have been his maxim. One only wishes he had been in doubt oftener.

For those who look for 'commitment' in the cinema in the new, fashionable sense of the term, the work of Ford—as well as of most great American directors prior to the 1960s—will have nothing to offer. But for those who look for art, for poetry, for a clean, healthy, robust attitude to life and human relationships, John Ford is among the most rewarding of directors. He was also unique in having won unreserved admiration from eminent film makers from all parts of the world—from Eisenstein in Soviet Russia, Kurosawa in Japan, Bergman in Sweden, and Orson Welles in the USA.

There is little doubt that this admiration was based primarily on the genre that Ford perfected. Along with slapstick comedy, the Western is the least literary of film genres. No wonder Ford's genius for pure cinema shone most luminously in it. For those who have a resistance to the genre itself, as well as for those who are only concerned with Subject Matter and Its Relevance to the Contemporary Scene—Ford's Westerns will remain a closed book. It would also be difficult to convey the greatness of Ford to someone who can only see what lies on the surface of a film; in other words, the aspect which is conveyed adequately in a screenplay. Ford's real achievement always transcends the literary framework. Plot and character are not what especially distinguish films like *Wagonmaster*, *The Sun Shines Bright*, or *My Darling Clementine*. The distinction consists, as in all great film makers, in the manner of telling the stories; in how Ford uses his tools, how he stages his actions and photographs them, where he places his camera, how the shots and the scenes follow one another, how the pace and the pulse of the film derive from the cutting. Among other things, Ford was a master of the static shot, of the 'telling' composition. There is rarely any movement of the camera within a shot unless it happens to be part of a larger action. This is a method which lies at the other extreme from, say, Orson Welles. One can say that in a Ford film the camera is a sensitive observer, always sure of the best viewpoint, while in Welles it is a dexterous participant, exploring all manner of viewpoints.

Much of the best things in a Ford film has the mysterious, indefinable quality of poetry. Because some of them appear casual—even accidental—it is difficult to realise how much experience and mastery lie behind them. Let me describe one such moment from the film *Fort Apache*. Two men stand talking on the edge of a deep ravine. There is a broken bottle lying alongside. One man gives it a casual kick and sends it flying over the edge. A few seconds later, in a gap in the conversation, the sound track registers the faintest of clinks. That's all. This is the sort of thing that belongs uniquely to the cinema. What it does is to invest a casual moment with poetic significance. Those who look for 'meaning' here, whether symbolic or literary, and are disappointed not to find it, are obviously unaware of what makes for poetry in the cinema. All the best Ford films are full of such poetic details, which, taken in conjunction with the sweep and vigour of the action sequences, give the films their satisfying richness.

A professional film maker to the core, Ford had remained distinctly aloof from the critical reaction to his work. He had been accused, often rightly, of sentimentality, of excessive proneness to nostalgia, of readiness to yield to commercial pressures. Nothing ever seemed to touch him or ruffle the serenity of his convictions. I suspect he had been too busy making films to bother. And not only about critics, but also about other directors and their work, least of all about young directors who were branching out in directions unexplored by himself. More than just indifference or preoccupation, one suspects here an inflexibility of mind which refused to accommodate alternative approaches to film making. Let me record here an instance of Ford's encounter with a young film maker fifteen years ago. Lindsay Anderson—whose adulation of Ford amounted almost to deification—had just made an hour-long documentary called *Every Day Except Christmas*, which showed what went on behind the scenes at London's famous Covent Garden Market. It was a fine, poetic film, primarily a film of mood, vaguely akin to Ford in its images of working-class camaraderie, but on the whole a very different kettle of fish. John Ford happened to be

in town, and Lindsay was anxious to show his film to his
mentor. A screening was arranged, and Ford was persuaded
to come after having been told who made the film and
what it was about. Ford was well aware of the high
regard in which his work was held by this young critic-
turned-film maker. At the screening, Lindsay sat next to
the Master. For half an hour after the film commenced,
Ford said not a word. Then, just as the conviction had
begun to grow in the *chela* that the *guru* had succumbed
to the spell of the film, Ford turned to Lindsay and said:
'Now, when are we going to see those goddam vegetables?'

1973

Index